Rome

Forevertown

Shadows fall on fallen stones that once held up the sky
Being there I felt at home, they've fallen, so have I
Now you look out your window, as the stars fall like snow
You're waiting for someone who will never show

And I can still recall the way you looked that night
We walked the silent streets until the red sunrise
The memory of your face is like the memory of that place
Calling me back to Forevertown

So you're waiting by the phone, as your heart turns to stone
And I live in the past, hoping this memory will last

Light reflects into my eyes like waking from a dream
Washed away into the past like all the years those streets have seen
But I will never let this feeling go
Even if no one will ever know

Now the place where I live can never be my home
No American skyline could replace Buonarroti's dome
Where the warm breeze blows down from the hills that surround
My heart's true home, Forevertown

Once upon a time I dared to dream of you and I
I fantasized that I would save your life
But now I can't remember how I ever lost track of you
Yet I know that's when I lost my spirit, too.

So you're waiting by the phone, as your heart turns to stone
And I live in the past, trying to make this feeling last

—Jim L. Papandrea/Remember Rome

Rome

A Pilgrim's Guide to the Eternal City

JAMES L. PAPANDREA
with photography by the author

CASCADE *Books* • Eugene, Oregon

ROME
A Pilgrim's Guide to the Eternal City

Copyright © 2012 James L. Papandrea. All rights reserved. Except for brief quotations in critical publications or reviews, no part of this book may be reproduced in any manner without prior written permission from the publisher. Write: Permissions, Wipf and Stock Publishers, 199 W. 8th Ave., Suite 3, Eugene, OR 97401.

Cascade Books
An Imprint of Wipf and Stock Publishers
199 W. 8th Ave., Suite 3
Eugene, OR 97401

www.wipfandstock.com

isbn 13: 978-1-61097-268-0

All photographs copyright © 2012 James L. Papandrea. All rights reserved.

Cataloging-in-Publication data:

Papandrea, James Leonard

    Rome : a pilgrim's guide to the eternal city / James L. Papandrea.

    x + 224 p. ; 23 cm.

    ISBN 13: 978-1-61097-268-0

1. Pilgrims and pilgrimages—Italy—Rome. 2. Rome (Italy)—Description—Guide-books. 3. Rome (Italy)—Buildings, structures, etc.—Guide-books. 4. Rome—Antiquities. I. Title.

DG804 P15 2012

Manufactured in the U.S.A.

*To my wife, Susie: my Co-traveler on the Journey of Life
Rome will always be our town*

There are many good women, but you surpass them all.
Proverbs 31:29

Contents

Acknowledgments | ix

Chapter 1
The Eternal City | 1

Chapter 2
The Ruins of a Fallen Empire | 12
    The Area of the Roman Forum and the Palatine Hill
    The Imperial Fora
    Roman Temples and Other Monuments
    The Museums

Chapter 3
Holy Ground | 53
    Where the Martyrs Died
    Where the Martyrs Were Buried

Chapter 4
The Churches of Rome | 80
    Looking Up to Heaven: The Apse Mosaics
    San Clemente
    Santa Croce in Gerusalemme
    Santa Pudenziana
    San Lorenzo Fuori le Mura
    Santa Sabina
    San Pietro in Vincoli
    Santi Cosma e Damiano
    Santa Maria in Cosmedin
    Santa Prassede
    Santa Cecilia
    San Benedetto

    Santa Maria in Trastevere
    Santa Maria del Popolo
    Sant' Agostino
    Santa Maria Maggiore
    San Paolo Fuori le Mura
    San Giovanni in Laterano
    San Pietro (St. Peter's and the Vatican)

Chapter 5
Walking Tours of Rome | 203

Appendix A: Coming Back to the Twenty-First Century | 213
Apeendix B:
    Chart: Rome Timeline | 217
    Map: The Roman Forum and Imperial Fora | 220
    Map: The Churches of Rome and Other Important Sites | 222

Acknowledgments

I WOULD LIKE TO thank my parents, who brought me to Rome for the first time at the age of fifteen. It was then that my life-long love affair with the Eternal City began. I would also like to thank Professors James Packer, Ili Nagy, and the good folks at the American Academy in Rome. My summer at the AAR was a life-changing experience. Special thanks to my good friends at Wipf and Stock/Cascade, for believing in this book (which was originally to be titled *Romesick: Making Your Pilgrimage to the Eternal City a Spiritual Homecoming*), Brooke Lester, for our conversations about the horns of Moses, and to Rich Vetrano for creating the excellent maps. Finally, I would like to thank the students, friends and family who have accompanied me to Rome, listened to me lecture, and learned to understand the true meaning of the words, "It's just around the corner." To all those who, like me, have come to think of Rome as their true home—you know what it's like when you're away too long and you start to feel . . . Romesick.

Chapter 1

The Eternal City

INTRODUCTION

THE BEST WAY TO go to Rome as a pilgrim (as opposed to a tourist) is to make a conscious effort to connect with the roots of the Christian faith in the city. Human beings have always had a sense that some places are holy ground, usually because something significant happened at that site. There is no place on earth, apart from the Holy Land itself, that has a greater connection to the earliest Christians than the city of Rome. Our goal as pilgrims, then, is to be in those places, stand on holy ground, walk on their stones, touch their walls, and see some of the very same things that they saw. When you go to Rome, you will be in those places where the songs of the first Christians echoed. You will walk where the apostles Peter and Paul walked. And you will feel the presence of that great cloud of witnesses, many of whom died rather than give up their faith.

This book, therefore, will focus on the churches and important sites of the world of the earliest Christians. This is not a tribute to the grandeur of a triumphant church as an institution, it is more an attempt to make a tangible connection to the Christians themselves through the places where they lived, worshiped, died, and were buried. Consequently, the church with which we are connecting is the church that belongs to all Christians. This book, and the kind of pilgrimage it will hopefully facilitate, is meant for Christians of any denomination, because the early church of Rome is in many ways the roots of the whole Christian family tree.

Of course it would be impossible to survey every church in Rome, so I have chosen what I believe are the most important ones, based on my experience studying in Rome and leading tours in Rome. In order to facilitate the spiritual nature of a pilgrimage, prayers are included along with the description of each church. These prayers would be appropriate to help you connect with earliest Christianity in each space, and in many cases, the prayers themselves are prayers that might have been prayed by the first Christians in that place. In most cases, I have also included prayers for the intercession of the saints to whom the holy places are dedicated, for those Christians whose traditions include this type of prayer.

In this book I will usually refer to relative chronology by centuries. So it is important to keep in mind that, for example, the third century is the 200s, because the dates of the first century have only two digits. Therefore, the fourth century is the 300s, the fifth century is the 400s, and so on. I will use the abbreviations "CE" to refer to dates of the Christian, or Common Era, the equivalent of AD (*Anno Domini*, the Year of the Lord); and "BCE" for Before the Common Era. Most dates, however, are of the Common Era, and any date without a distinction can be assumed to be CE (AD). For the cases when we are talking of the time before the Common Era (BCE), remember that the years count down (backwards), so that the smaller numbers are actually later, counting down as they move toward the "zero" point (there is no zero year). This means that the fifth century BCE (the 400s BCE) is *before* the fourth century BCE (the 300s BCE). See the Rome timeline chart at the end of the book for an overview of important events related to the history of Rome and the Roman Christians.

It is my hope that you will read this book before you leave for Rome, and bring it with you for reference along the way. Also, take a look at the Romesick websites (www.Romesick.com and www.Romesick.org) to see color versions of the pictures in the book, as well as more pictures of Rome and its churches.

CHRISTIAN PILGRIMAGE, JUBILEE, AND HOLY DOORS

The tradition of Christian pilgrimage to Rome goes back to the time when it was impossible for Christians of the west to travel to the Holy Land. In Rome, they could find important sites of the faith, including the places where the apostles Peter and Paul were martyred and buried. They could visit the places where the other heroes of the faith were buried, and in being close to their remains, they felt closer to God. Pilgrims to Rome were called *Romei*, as though they were somehow spiritually citizens of the city. In the Middle Ages, the tradition of the Jubilee year emerged, encouraging Christians from all over the world to journey to Rome. In the Old Testament, Jubilee meant the forgiveness of debt, and that idea came to be combined with the concept of pilgrimage as a symbol of return from exile. So the one who makes a pilgrimage in a Jubilee year is symbolically returning to God, like a prodigal coming home. Pilgrims arriving in Rome would enter one of the four main basilicas through a special door, called a Holy Door, symbolizing their "homecoming," to receive forgiveness and reconciliation with God. Now there is a Jubilee year every twenty-five years, and the Holy Doors are opened to welcome pilgrims. There is a Holy Door on each of the four papal basilicas, Santa Maria Maggiore (St. Mary Major), San Paulo Fuori le Mura (St. Paul Outside the Walls), San Giovanni in Laterano (St. John Lateran), and San Pietro (St. Peter in the Vatican). The Holy Door on St. Peter's is opened by the pope on Christmas Eve before a Jubilee year in an interesting ceremony that goes back to the year 1500; it includes knocking on the door three times with a special hammer. It is left open for the year of the Jubilee, to be closed (and bricked over) the next Christmas Eve. The other three Holy Doors are opened by cardinals. For those pilgrims who pass through a Holy Door, their pilgrimage is accepted as an act of penance, an outward sign of inward repentance for sin.

A NOTE ON ALMSGIVING

Just like the ancient pilgrims, you will no doubt encounter beggars in Rome. Many of them seem as though they are homeless, though that may not be the case. There are gypsies and others who make their living begging and pooling their money at the end of the day. That in itself is not necessarily a reason to refuse to give; however, the point is that not everyone who begs is in danger of going without food that day. You may even notice some who carry signs in English—signs that were obviously printed from a computer!

Almsgiving is an ancient tradition in many religions, and in the earliest Christian documents almsgiving is praised as a form of ministry to the poor. Therefore, you are encouraged to make almsgiving a part of your pilgrimage experience. However, if you give money to every beggar you encounter (some of whom are sitting at the entrances to the churches) you would quickly run out of your vacation budget. Therefore, plan ahead for how you want to give to the poor of Rome. You are not a bad Christian if you pass up some opportunities to give. Plan ahead each day and keep some coins in a separate pocket, so that if you do choose to give, no one will see where you keep your money. You never know if a beggar might be working with a pickpocket. And under no circumstances should you ever buy anything from the vendors on the street who sell imitation designer purses, sunglasses, or anything laid out on cardboard boxes or sheets. Clergy in Rome are concerned that the vendors are being used to make money for organized crime and, thus, indirectly supporting the illegal drug trade and human trafficking.

OTHER PRACTICAL CONSIDERATIONS REGARDING TRAVEL IN ROME

As the reader can see, the purpose of this book is not to tell you which hotels are the best, or where to find a good restaurant (though you should stay away from any restaurant with a laminated menu with pictures of the meals on it). This is not a travel book, in that sense. Still, there are a few things to keep in mind when you are in such a global city as Rome.

Violent crime is not a great concern in Rome, however you need to watch out for pickpockets. At the very least, keep your money in a front pocket, not a back pocket. Any time someone is in your "personal space," keep a hand over the pocket with your money in it. Avoid crowded areas where you cannot control your personal space. Sometimes you can't help it, like when you're on the metro at rush hour (though avoid that if you can), but simply be aware that there are people who will take your money if you're not careful. Especially watch out for groups of children who approach you, sometimes carrying a newspaper, cardboard or something else to shove at you, distracting you while their cohorts go through your pockets. Should this happen, yell at them to go away, and walk quickly away from them. Also, if you see a political demonstration, avoid getting into the crowd. These demonstrations are usually not violent, however it's best to walk away from them and stay out of the situation.

Note that when you visit the churches, make sure to have some coins handy, since many of the churches are dimly lit, but have coin-operated lights so that you can see the artwork better.

Finally, if at all possible, make sure to attend church while in Rome. Roman Catholic Mass for English speakers is at Santa Susanna (the Roman Catholic church for Americans) and a few other places. There are Protestant churches in Rome as well, and a few minutes research on the internet should lead you to the church of your denomination in Rome (or the nearest equivalent). Some of the Protestant churches don't look like churches from the outside, so be aware that you might be looking for a worship space built into an existing building. The Methodist church for English speakers is Ponte Sant' Angelo. The Episcopal church is Saint Paul's Within the Walls.

THE TITLE CHURCHES

The concept of a "Title Church" applies to the tradition that there are twenty-five oldest churches in Rome, each one the site of an original "title," or property held by the early Christians of the city. These are believed to be the places where there were early Christian congregations who gathered for worship in a home, apartment, or warehouse space. We have to keep in mind that before the fourth century, there were no *churches*, no buildings built specifically for Christian worship. There may have been buildings converted into worship space, and there certainly were houses and apartments remodeled to accommodate Christian worship, but you could not walk down the street and see *a church*.

It is well known that the first Christians worshiped in homes. In the apostle Paul's letter to the Romans (written in about the year 57), Paul seems to mention five house-church congregations in Rome, though there may have been more already by that time. Apparently, by the late first century there were twenty-five congregations, probably segregated by social class, language (Greek vs. Latin), and geographically within the city. According to tradition, Anacletus (bishop of Rome from 76–88) ordained priests and appointed them over the twenty-five churches. The number of house-church congregations then grew steadily until the middle of the third century when we hear that there were about fifty of them.

If a congregation was meeting in a private home, the owner of the home sometimes remodeled parts of the house so that it would accommodate more worshipers. In some places, baptismal fonts were added. The original owner of the property (the holder of the "title") may have been the first "pastor" of the congregation, but in many cases, the owner of the property or some other prominent leader of the congregation was martyred for his or her faith. When that happened, the martyr was buried on private land, either associated with the house, or more likely on land owned by the church's patron outside the city (there was a law against burials within the city walls). To honor the martyr's sacrifice, the congregation (still not a building) was remembered as the church of that martyr. And since martyrs were considered to have guaranteed their place in heaven with a baptism in their own blood, they were called holy, so that a church associated with a martyr named Cecilia, for example, became the church of the holy Cecilia, or the church of Saint Cecilia.

Some of the martyrs, or their families, eventually left the property in question to the care of the Christian community. Even before the church as an institution could legally own property, the Christians controlled some house churches where no one actually lived (or perhaps the priest lived there), and even some land outside the city walls that became the Christian cemeteries, the catacombs. Someone who had been a patron of the church, once martyred, became a spiritual patron of the Christian community. Based on Jesus' words in Matthew 10:19–20, the martyrs were believed to have been inspired by the Holy Spirit to witness to the faith at the risk of their lives. And since it was clear that they were living the life of the resurrection in the presence of their Lord, the early Christians asked for their intercession. Furthermore, it became desirable to be buried near the martyrs, and so the catacombs grew as the Christian community buried its beloved departed in close proximity to those who were considered the pillars of the faith. More will be said about the catacombs below, the point for now is that small chapels called *martyria* (singular: *martyrium*) grew up at the sites of important burials. The pilgrims would then visit these *martyria* to pay their respects to the martyrs, to pray, and to seek spiritual guidance for the journey of life.

The sites of earliest Christian worship in Rome, then, are the sites of some of the earliest house churches, and some of the *martyria* built at the catacombs. Over time, some of the original house churches were renamed for a later martyr who became more famous (which is why it is impossible to connect the congregations mentioned by Paul with any particular title churches). In the fourth century, the first Christian emperor, Constantine, gave money for the building of the first Christian basilicas on the sites of the catacombs, or the house churches. Later the popes of the fifth and sixth centuries embellished or remodeled the buildings. In the early Middle Ages, the martyrs' remains were brought into the basilicas within the city walls, prompting the addition of side altars to accommodate the many saints. This was done for various reasons, including the threat of desecration by barbarian invasions, and to facilitate the visits of pilgrims.

The twenty-five traditional title churches are (in no particular order): Santa Pudenziana, Santa Prassede, San Clemente, Santa Sabina, San Vitale, San Pietro in Vincoli, Santa Cecilia, San Crisogono, Santa Maria in Trastevere, San Martino ai Monti, San Sisto, Santi Giovanni e Paolo, Quattro Coronati, Santi Marcello e Pietro, San Eusebio, Santa Susanna, San Marcello, San Lorenzo in Lucina, San Lorenzo in Damaso, San Marco, Santa Anastasia, Santa Prisca, Santa Balbina, Santi Nereo e Achilleo (in the catacombs of Domitilla, later moved near the Baths of Caracalla), and San Trypho (replaced by Sant' Agostino). Not all of these are included in this book because in some cases they are very difficult to get into, and in other cases little or nothing is left of the ancient church. However, if one were to spend an extended time in Rome, the others are worth tracking down.

The churches included in this book are presented in as close to chronological order as possible, however one must keep in mind that every church has many layers of history. In each case, the story of the church and its background will be given (as far as we know), but always with an emphasis on the earliest Christian witness in a particular place. Note that the oldest things are below street level. It is a fact of history that street level rises over time (I'm told the mountains are getting shorter to make up for it, but other than that I can't explain it). The point is that the older something is, it is usually lower than the newer layers above it. However keep in mind that Rome is a city built on hills, so when it comes to sites on the hills, sometimes older layers on the hill are above newer layers at the foot of the hill.

The Church of San Vitale, with Fifth-Century Façade Below Street Level

Finally, a note about the popes is in order. The pope is first and foremost the Roman Catholic bishop of Rome. Therefore, all popes are also the bishop of Rome, and when I mention them I will include the dates that they held the office of bishop. However, the office of bishop, and indeed the papacy, developed over time, so that while all popes are the bishop of Rome, it is not technically accurate to say that all bishops of Rome are popes in the way we think of the papacy. In other words, the earliest bishops of Rome held an office that was less administrative, and to a certain extent less authoritative than the office of bishop as it now exists. Even more so, the early bishops of Rome shared the title "Papa" (pope) with the bishops of other major cities, so that the first bishops we can call pope, in the sense of a singular authority who is the only one to carry that title, would probably be the bishops of the fifth century. Nevertheless, there are a few earlier bishops for whom the title is still appropriate, even if the bishops of other major cities would also have claimed the title at the same time. Therefore, I will refer to bishops of the fourth century as popes as well, since the title was used at least as early as Marcellinus, who died in 304, and whose burial inscription includes an abbreviation that designates him as Pope. In addition, the apostle Peter is historically given the honor of being called the first bishop of Rome (and the first Pope), and although the office of bishop as we know it did not really exist yet in Peter's time, as an apostle, Peter certainly would have held the position of "overseer" in the Roman church, the same way John would have held that position over the churches of Asia Minor.

DEVOTIONAL LEGENDS

There is much legendary material from the early church, especially from the times of persecution. Many documents were written to honor the martyrs of the faith, some of them are almost entirely legendary, others have layers of pious fiction added to a historical core. I have not always included legendary material that one might find in other sources, attempting instead to stay as close as possible to what is historically verifiable. However, there is a lot of information that may be based on oral tradition, and was only written down later, which nevertheless has become part of the story of some of the early Christian sites. In those cases where the information is not based on verifiable sources, I will usually begin by saying, "According to tradition . . ." or "It is said that . . ." This is the reader's cue to take the tradition with a grain of salt. Still, the purpose of this book is to encourage your faith and facilitate the spiritual nature of your pilgrimage, so I will include some of those stories of the church that are edifying, as long as they are not (in my opinion) too far-fetched.

At this point it will suffice to give three examples which will not be mentioned in the main body of the book below, but that are relatively famous sites associated with early Christianity in Rome. The first is the so-called *Quo Vadis?* church. This is actually a small chapel on the Appian Way, commemorating the supposed site of a vision of the apostle Peter. The story of the vision comes from the legendary *Acts of Peter*, and it was made famous by the 1951 film, *Quo Vadis?*. The legend says that the apostle Peter had been convinced by the Christian community to leave Rome to escape the persecution of the emperor Nero (this would have been about the year 64 or 65). As he walked out of the city along the Appian Way, he saw a vision of Jesus walking toward him. He asked Jesus, *Quo Vadis, Domine?* (Where are you going, Lord?). Jesus replied that he was going to Rome to be crucified again, and this was a sign to Peter that it was his destiny to return to Rome, where he would be martyred by crucifixion. The site where Peter met the Lord is marked by the

Quo Vadis? chapel, which is actually the church of Santa Maria in Palmis, named after the footprints of Jesus that mark the spot where he supposedly stood. The marble in the floor with the footprints in it is a copy—the original, supposedly miraculous, footprints are in a stone in the church of San Sebastiano (over the catacomb of the same name). The present *Quo Vadis?* chapel dates from the seventeenth century; however, there has been a chapel on that site at least since the ninth century, and it has been a popular pilgrim site.

Another site is the so-called Mamertine Prison. This is the supposed place of the incarceration of the apostles Peter and Paul (though not necessarily at the same time). If the apostle Paul had really been held here, it would have to have been his assumed second imprisonment (see Paul's "last words" in 2 Timothy 3:10–11; 4:6–22.) There was a prison here, called the Tullianum, where political prisoners were held and sometimes simply left to die of starvation (including prisoners of war, who were thrown into this sewer-like cell after being displayed in the triumphal parades of victorious generals). However there is no evidence that either Peter or Paul was ever held here. There is a story that when Peter was in this prison, a miraculous spring of water bubbled up so that he could baptize his fellow prisoners and his guards. This story is certainly not true, since the spring in question is attested in literary sources long before Peter ever came to Rome. On the other hand, regardless of whether Peter or Paul was ever here, it is likely that some Christians died here. Unfortunately, however, it has recently been turned into a tourist trap and stripped of any spiritual value it may have had.

On the other hand, the church of Santa Maria in Via Lata is worth a visit, as it is the traditional site of the apostle Paul's house arrest in Rome (Acts 28:16). In excavations under the church, there is an ancient house, long venerated as the home of St. Luke the Evangelist. For a while in the Middle Ages it was turned into a monastery, but now it is a memorial to the ministry of the apostles in Rome.

A WORD ABOUT RELICS

On your pilgrimage to Rome, you will see many relics (from the Latin word, *relicta*, meaning things that are left, or that remain). Some of these relics are the physical remains of the heroes of the faith—literally body parts of the martyrs. Other relics are tangible elements of the story of early Christianity, things from the early church that were saved by Christians throughout the centuries because they were highly valued artifacts of their ancestors in the faith. Sometimes these relics would themselves become the object of veneration, and the sites that housed them would become important destinations for pilgrims. You will, no doubt, see relics of varying veracity—in other words, you will wonder how some of them could possibly be what they claim to be. Some will seem to have a high probability of being what they are presented to be, others not so much. With some relics, even the Roman Catholic Church is apparently reluctant to stand by the traditional claims, as evidenced by the fact that they are relegated to places of lesser honor, such as a crowded room in a small museum in the basement of a church. In any case, I encourage you, without suspending a healthy skepticism, to see the relics for what they are: devotional icons, windows into the world of the early Christians that will hopefully enhance your connection to your ancestors in the faith, as well as the spiritual experience of being in Rome. To that end, this book will simply describe the relics as they are presented according to tradition, and not attempt to sort out which ones are "real." The reality of the relic, as icon, is up to the observer, if he or she is willing to see beyond it to what it symbolizes. The early Christians believed that since the holy ones (saints) who left these relics behind are eternally with God, being close to the relics made them feel as though they were closer to God. But these relics were not worshiped, since worship would imply that they were an end in themselves. The relics were only venerated, as a means to an end, which was access to the Divine. Regardless of what one thinks of the historical reality of the relics and the effectiveness of their veneration, they remain one possible way to connect with those Christians who have gone before us, and through them, to connect with God.

Chapter 2

The Ruins of a Fallen Empire

Fallen! Fallen is Babylon the Great! (Rev 14:8; 18:2). When the apostle John heard these words, they were a prophetic reference to the Roman Empire, which was predicted to fall. And fall it did. Yet the remains of the empire (and the republic that preceded it) are all around Rome. Being in Rome, one is surrounded by the "relics" of the empire. In order to make a connection with the earliest Christians in the city of Rome, we have to understand the world in which they lived. We'll do that by seeing (and

The Roman Forum

touching) some of the ancient remnants of the empire—monuments and buildings that the early Christians would have walked past every day are still to be seen in Rome, at least in pieces. In any case, one cannot go to Rome without visiting the most famous sites that have become iconic of the city itself.

THE AREA OF THE ROMAN FORUM AND THE PALATINE HILL

The Roman forum and the adjacent Palatine Hill were the site of the first inhabitation in the area, before Rome was even a city, let alone an empire. Evidence of tombs dating back to the tenth century BCE have been found in the forum, and evidence of huts from the iron age (eighth century BCE) has been found on the hill. According to tradition, the city of Rome was founded in 753 BCE, and was ruled by kings until the time of the Republic, which began in 509 BCE. During the time of the Republic, the forum became the marketplace, and eventually evolved into the center of business and politics, as well as religious ceremony. Triumphal parades and funeral processions would travel along the main road through the forum, called the *Via Sacra*. Originally the sewer ran in an open ditch through the forum, but by the first century BCE, it was covered and ran underneath the square. If you look carefully, you may still see where the sewer ran beneath the paving stones. The lowest level that one can now walk on is the street level of the republican forum (in the mid-first century CE the street level was raised to the level on which the triumphal arches now stand). However, fires in the third century BCE and the first century BCE destroyed much of the earliest monuments, so that most of what you now see comes from a renovation begun by Julius Caesar, and completed by Augustus and the emperors of the first century CE.

Augustus was the first true emperor, and it was he who successfully converted the republic into an empire at the end of the first century BCE. By the time of the birth of Christ, the forum was transformed from a gathering place for the people into the political and military nerve center of the empire. Eventually it even had a dress code, allowing only those wearing the senatorial toga. However, more fires and ransacking by invading barbarians would cause the republican forum to decline in favor of new fora set up by the emperors. By the Middle Ages, the main forum had become a quarry for building materials. In the ninth century, an earthquake and floods caused the sewer to overflow, turning the area into a swamp. Eventually, it was covered by layers of dirt and debris, and it became a cattle pasture and an abandoned field where poor squatters built shacks in which to live. The location of the old heart of Rome was all but forgotten, and drawings of the area from the 19th century show only the tops of the tallest monuments sticking out of the ground. When the forum and its historical treasures were rediscovered, it was excavated to reveal what you see today. We'll begin at the western end of the forum, and work our way toward the east. See the map, "The Roman Forum and Imperial Fora," at the end of the book for the exact locations of the monuments.

The Temple of Saturn

Beginning at the southwest corner of the forum, we see the imposing façade of the Temple of Saturn. Originally built in 497 BCE, it was rebuilt after a fire in 42 BCE, and the front row of columns still standing are from an addition by the emperor Diocletian at the turn of the fourth century CE. Diocletian was the emperor at the beginning of the Great Persecution, so these columns were put up at about the same time as the worst

The Temple of Saturn

persecution of the church in the empire's history. The inscription across the top is from this time and says, *The Senate and People of Rome restored what was consumed by fire.* In addition to being a pagan temple dedicated to the god Saturn, this was also the treasury of ancient Rome. The temple itself would have served as a storehouse for the imperial treasury, Rome's version of Fort Knox. Near the base of the temple is a remnant of an ancient column called the *Miliarium Aureum.* You may have heard the expression that "all roads lead to Rome." For the Romans, this column was the precise point at which all roads converged, and therefore it would be the point from which the governors of provinces would be sent out to take up their posts.

Portico of the Gods in Agreement (Portico of the Assenting Gods)

Behind the Temple of Saturn is a row of columns from the reign of Julian "the Apostate" (361–363 CE), the only non-Christian emperor after Constantine. The portico was part of a temple that was meant to be a kind of pantheon, dedicated to all the gods and housing statues of all the important gods of ancient Rome. This was the last pagan temple built in Rome.

The Temple of Vespasian and Titus

There is not much left of this temple, other than three standing columns of one corner. The temple was built to honor the emperors Vespasian and Titus, by their successor Domitian, who was Vespasian's son and Titus' brother. Vespasian and Titus were the generals who led the war in Judea, and Titus was the one responsible for the siege of Jerusalem and the destruction of the Jerusalem temple in 70 CE. It was during the reign of Domitian, in 95 CE, when the apostle John was exiled to the island of Patmos where he wrote the book of Revelation.

The Arch of Septimius Severus

Next we come to the Arch of Septimius Severus, who reigned as emperor 193–211 CE. The arch was built to commemorate Severus' victory over the Parthians (the Persians), a long time enemy of Rome, and the relief sculptures on the arch show scenes from the battles. The arch is meant to represent a kind of gateway, through which the triumph, or victory

Rome

parade, of an emperor would process (though in reality an arch might be built long after the fact). One has to imagine the triumphal arch as a glorified statue base, since it would have had on top a statue of the emperor in the *quadriga*, or four-horse chariot. In the year 202 CE, Septimius Severus issued an imperial edict authorizing the persecution of Christians. This arch was built in the year 203, the same year of the famous martyrdoms of Perpetua and Felicitas in Carthage, North Africa. Severus had two sons, Caracalla and Geta. When Severus died, Caracalla murdered his brother Geta so that he could be the sole emperor. If you look closely at the inscription on the arch, you can see that Caracalla had Geta's name chiseled off, a posthumous sentence known as *damnatio memoriae*, or the condemnation of the very memory of a man.

The Arch of Septimius Severus

The Curia

The one building of the forum that appears to be most intact is the *curia*, or the senate house. The senate was the ruling body of the Roman

Republic, having expelled the last of the kings in 509 BCE. The original *curia* on this site was built by Julius Caesar, though he would never see it finished. The present building, however is from the turn of the fourth century, from the reign of Diocletian. Note the original marble floor from Diocletian's time. The senators would sit on either side of the hall, and voting was done by moving to one side or the other. However, by the time of Diocletian, most senators never showed up here, preferring instead the safety of their country estates where they were not in danger of saying the wrong thing and angering the emperor. Those senators who did meet to rubber stamp the emperor's wishes often met in the palace on the hill, an implicit admission that the spirit of the senate was already dead. The main niche of the *curia* held a statue of the goddess Victoria (victory), which remained until it was removed in the fifth century CE, against the protestations of the last of the pagan senators. Like many ancient buildings, this one was turned into a church in the seventh century, only to be decommissioned later. The original bronze doors of the *curia* are now on the cathedral of Rome, San Giovanni in Laterano.

The Roman Basilicas: Basilica Aemilia and Basilica Julia

The word, "basilica" refers to a type of architecture, usually a large rectangular building with porticoes, used for meetings related to law and commerce. The name probably comes from the Greek word for king, and may reflect an early use as the audience hall of the kings. You may be familiar with the use of the word, "basilica" in reference to churches, but that's because the earliest church buildings were built on the basilica plan. In other words, the earliest buildings made specifically for Christian worship used an architectural plan that was already known to work well for gathering large groups of people. Sometimes, the basilica would have a large rounded niche at one end, called an *apse*. Originally, the apse might have held a statue of a god or emperor, but when the design was taken over for Christian use, the apse became the focal point of the worship service, the place where the priest presided over the Eucharist. Eventually, the transept was added to make the building cross-shaped, and the "arms" of the transept became side chapels, sacristies, or baptisteries. The altar was then moved out to the center of the cross. Thus the word basilica shifted from a place where one might meet an earthly king to a place where we meet the King of kings. However, the pre-Christian Roman basilicas did not have a transept—they were simply large rectangles.

The two main basilicas of the republican forum were the Basilica Aemilia and the Basilica Julia. All that remains today is the floor plan and the remains of some of the columns. The basilicas were destroyed during an invasion of the Goths in the year 410. The Basilica Aemilia is next to the *curia* (on the right hand side of the forum if you're facing the Temple of Saturn). It was built in 179 BCE to be a place for business transactions. Across the forum from the Basilica Aemilia is the Basilica Julia, built by Julius Caesar to be a new courthouse. Apparently, those waiting for their time in court sat on the marble steps and passed the time by playing games, something like a Roman version of tic-tac-toe. See if you can find the remains of the game boards they scratched into the marble.

The Temple of Castor and Pollux

Next to the Basilica Julia, opposite from the Temple of Saturn, is the remains of the Temple of Castor and Pollux (also known as the *Dioscuri*, kind of like the twins of Gemini). The temple was built in the fifth century BCE to commemorate supposed divine intervention in a battle of 499 BCE, in which the Romans defeated the Latins to unite the two tribes and solidify the republic. The temple was rebuilt in the second century BCE and the outer columns were added in the first century BCE, but only three of the original thirty-four columns are standing today. Statues of Castor and Pollux also watch over the ramp leading to the Capitoline Hill.

The Church of Santa Maria Antiqua

Behind the Temple of Castor and Pollux was once the Athenaeum built by the emperor Hadrian (reigned 117–138 CE). As the name implies, the Athenaeum was meant to embody the learning of ancient Greece, and was in effect a kind of college, complete with a famous library. In the sixth century CE, part of the Athenaeum was turned into a church dedicated to the Virgin Mary. The church was later buried in a landslide of rubble from the hillside, and eventually rediscovered and excavated. At the present time, it is closed to the public, though it will be reopened at some point and it is worth checking to see whether you can get in.

The Ruins of a Fallen Empire

The Temple of the Divine Julius

In the middle of the forum, between the Temple of Castor and Pollux and the Basilica Aemilia, is the Temple of the Divine Julius. After the assassination of Julius Caesar in 44 BCE, a civil war ensued, which ended with the victory of Caesar's nephew Octavian. In the year 29 BCE, Octavian was granted a new name by the senate, *Augustus*, which means "auspicious," or even, "endorsed by the augurs (soothsayers)." To solidify his own position as the new emperor, Augustus used the occasion of a passing comet to say that this was the spirit of his uncle Julius Caesar, who was now a god. Thus he convinced the senate to declare Julius Caesar divine, a move that was new for the Romans, but was based on the precedent of the claims of Egyptian pharaohs. Thus the altar where Caesar's remains had been cremated became a temple to him as a god. Two triumphal arches of Augustus once flanked the temple, commemorating his victory over Marc Antony and Cleopatra (on the south side) and over the Parthians (on the north side of the temple).

The Temple of Antoninus and Faustina

Next to the Basilica Aemilia (on the other side of the entrance path) is the Temple of Antoninus and Faustina. It was originally built by the emperor Antoninus Pius (reigned 136–161 CE), to honor his wife Faustina. When he died, it was also dedicated to him. Antoninus Pius was the emperor to whom Justin Martyr addressed his *First Apology*. He was also the emperor at the time of the martyrdom of the bishop Polycarp of Smyrna. The remains of the base of the altar can still be seen on the steps. Note that pagan temples had their altars on the outside, and often only the priests of the cult would actually enter the temple. It was the Christian church that moved worship to the inside of the sacred building, which is why many churches look rather plain on the outside, but are ornately decorated on the inside. This particular temple was turned into a church in the twelfth century CE, but it is no longer in service. Notice the level of the door of the church—this was ground level in the twelfth century. This means that part of the columns were below ground level. In 1342, an attempt was made to pull down the columns so that they could be used to renovate the church of San Giovanni in Laterano, however the workers apparently did not know just how much of the columns were below ground. You can still see the grooves at the top of the columns from the ropes used to try to pull the columns down.

The Temple of Jupiter Stator (Romulus)

A little farther down from the Temple of Antoninus and Faustina is the smaller round temple of Jupiter Stator, also known as the Temple of Romulus. This is an ancient temple (third century BCE), eventually rebuilt by the would-be emperor Maxentius during the time he occupied Rome in the fourth century CE. It is said that in the year 310 he renamed it the Temple of Romulus to dedicate it to his infant son Romulus (named after one of the traditional founders of Rome) who had died and was proclaimed a god in 309. It is also said that the ancient lock in the original bronze doors still works. The back of the temple is now part of the Church of Santi Cosma e Damiano, which we will visit from outside the forum. If the entrance to the temple is not open, the inside of the temple can be seen through glass at the back of the church.

The Domus Rex Sacrorum

In the middle of the forum, between the temples of Antoninus and Faustina and Jupiter Stator on one side, and the House of the Vestals on the other, is the *Domus Rex Sacrorum* (sometimes called the *Domus Publica*). The name Domus Rex Sacrorum implies that it was the house of the "king of sacred things," or the high priest of Roman religion, the Pontifex Maximus. It is said that Julius Caesar once lived here when he held that office.

The Temple of Vesta and the House of the Vestals

The round temple in the middle of the forum is unmistakable. It is the temple of Vesta, and the center of the cult of the famous Vestal Virgins. The temple was round to imitate the ancient huts of the first inhabitants of Rome, and it housed the sacred flame that represented the hearth (and the very life) of the Roman people. There was no statue of the goddess Vesta in the temple, only the fire, however it was said that below the temple was kept a statue of the goddess Minerva, one of the idols supposedly brought to Rome by Aeneas when he fled Troy. The Vestal Virgins were priestesses chosen by lot by the Pontifex Maximus, the high priest of all

Rome's cults. There were six of them at any one time, taken between the ages of six and ten from the wealthiest families of Rome (originally they were said to have been the daughters of the kings of Rome). The Vestals dedicated themselves to the cult for thirty years, after which they were released from service and could marry. A Vestal caught not being a virgin would be buried alive, since it was considered bad luck to spill their blood. Their hair was cut and they wore a wool cap with a white linen hood. It was the job of the Vestal Virgins always to keep the sacred fire burning, and if any let the fire go out, she would be whipped. However, they were given great social power, such that if they encountered a man on his way to be executed, the Vestals could pardon him if they so chose. They sat at a place of honor at the public games, along with the emperor. The original temple of Vesta burned down in the great fire of 64 CE, and was rebuilt by the emperor Nero (reigned 54–68 CE). It burned down on several other occasions, so that much of what you see today is later, including a significant reconstruction from the fascist era of the early twentieth century. The House of the Vestals is adjacent to the temple and includes a garden area surrounded by statues. The statues standing today are of prominent Vestals, but they are not in their original places. It is said that there is a statue base with the name chiseled off, except for the first initial C. This is said to be the base of a statue of the Vestal Claudia, who converted to Christianity and subsequently suffered *damnatio memoriae*.

The Basilica of Maxentius/Constantine

The largest of the forum's basilicas was begun by the general Maxentius, when he occupied Rome in the early fourth century. In the year 312 CE, Constantine defeated Maxentius in the battle at the Milvian Bridge on the outskirts of Rome, which solidified Constantine's power as emperor over the western half of the empire. This allowed Constantine to issue the Edict of Milan in 313 CE, legalizing Christianity. Also in the year 313, Constantine finished the basilica that his enemy had started. This was the largest vaulted hall of the ancient world, using an early form of flying buttresses. In fact, the architecture had some influence on the original design for St. Peter's basilica. A huge statue of Constantine, parts of which are now in the Capitoline Museum, was placed in the main apse. Constantine, as emperor, moved the most important functions of the government out of the *curia* to this building, though he would eventually move his

Rome

entire court to the eastern city of Byzantium, renaming it *Nova Roma*, or "New Rome." It was eventually also named after himself: Constantinople. One of the columns from the Basilica of Maxentius/Constantine is now in the piazza at the church of Santa Maria Maggiore.

The Arch of Titus

We are now at the opposite end of the forum from the Temple of Saturn and the Arch of Severus. Almost as a bookend with the Arch of Severus is the smaller Arch of Titus. The emperor Titus reigned 79–81 CE, but before he became the emperor, he was the general in charge of the legions that destroyed Jerusalem and its temple in 70. This triumphal arch was built by Titus' brother Domitian after his death and subsequent

The Arch of Titus

deification by the senate. The arch commemorates the victory in Judea, as well as the deification of Titus. If you look up into the vault of the arch, the sculpture depicts Titus being carried into the heavens by an eagle. On the inside of the arch, looking toward the north, is a frieze that shows Titus in a *quadriga*, led by the goddess Roma, the personification of Rome. Two men at the side of the chariot represent the senate (wearing a toga) and the people (shirtless). The juxtaposition of the senate and the people of Rome became a kind of shorthand for the empire itself, abbreviated in the acronym SPQR, which stands for *Senatus Popolusque Romanus*, the Senate and the People of Rome. The most famous part of this arch, though, is the frieze on the inside looking toward the south. There we see a depiction of the triumphal parade of Titus, showing off the spoils of war after the victory in Jerusalem. One can clearly see the menorah from the temple, and it has been suggested that the square image being carried by the soldiers is the ark of the covenant. It is interesting to note that soon after Titus became emperor (on the 24th of August in the year 79 CE), Mount Vesuvius erupted, destroying the cities of Pompeii and Herculaneum, which were favorites of the Roman elite. The arch was originally faced with marble, however not all the marble remains. You can see that the modern restorations purposely used different, simpler

The Triumph of Titus, Showing the Treasures of the Jerusalem Temple

materials so that the viewer can tell what parts are original (note how the top level is not as ornate, showing that it was rebuilt). In the Middle Ages, the arch was built into the fortress of a powerful family who used it as their front door.

The Temple of Venus and Roma

The last structure of the forum, and one of the largest temples of Rome, was actually a double temple—two temples back to back, built by the emperor Hadrian in the early second century CE. You'll get a better view from the Colosseum, since the temple facing the forum was built into the monastery and church of Santa Francesca Romana, also known as Santa Maria Nova (to distinguish it from Santa Maria Antiqua). There is a small museum called the *Antiquarium* within the monastery.

The Temple of Venus and Roma

The Palatine Hill

Going up the hill from the Arch of Titus, we come to the Palatine Hill, which became the home of the emperors, and from which we get our

English word, "palace." The earliest evidence of inhabitants on the Palatine goes back to the Iron-Age, specifically the mid-eighth century BCE, precisely the time when tradition says the city of Rome was founded. According to the myth, Rome was founded by twin brothers, Romulus and Remus, who were abandoned, but nursed by a wolf until they were found and raised by a shepherd. At the archaeological site, look for holes cut into the ground for the vertical posts used to make the Iron-Age huts. The so-called *Casa Romuli* (house of Romulus) was supposed to be on this site. In the republic, the area of the Palatine became a place where the wealthy built their homes, and when Augustus married his wife Livia, he chose to live in her home on the Palatine Hill as an intentional move to symbolically connect him to the mythical founders of Rome, and give the impression that he would be Rome's "second founder." Be sure to visit the House of Livia/Augustus to see the first-century BCE wall paintings, still vivid even after two thousand years. Other similar wall paintings are now in the National Museum at the Baths of Diocletian.

Augustus probably lived at the house of Livia while he was building a more impressive home on the Palatine Hill. The next emperor, Tiberius (reigned 14–37 CE), expanded it into a mansion that came to be called the *Domus Tiberiana* (house of Tiberius). The emperor Domitian turned it into what might be called a true palace, closing it off from public space so that the emperor would be shielded from the people. Eventually, the imperial palace took over the whole Palatine Hill. The great structures one can see from the other side of the hill (the Circus Maximus side) is the *Domus Severiana* (house of Severus), and is actually only the support structure for the expansion of the emperor Severus who ran out of hilltop. This expansion meant that the emperor could watch the races and other spectacles in the Circus Maximus from his balcony without mixing with the people. This was the home of all of the Roman emperors until Constantine moved his court (and indeed the capital of the empire) to the east. After that it was used by the emperors when visiting Rome, and by the western emperors who would be appointed to rule under the authority of the emperors in the east.

As you wander around the grounds of the imperial palaces, look for the foundation of a giant fountain with the shape of four Roman shields in a square pattern. There is also a long rectangular garden area with a semicircle at one end, with what looks like a small *circus*, or horse racetrack. This was not really a circus, but may have been a place for the training of horses. Also make sure to walk through the *cryptoporticus*, the

Rome

underground passageway where the emperor Caligula was assassinated in 41 CE.

There is also a spot where you can see below the floor—notice the space under the floor for the *hypocaust* system, by which fires could be lit below the floors to heat the buildings in cold weather. There is a small museum which focuses on the early inhabitation of the Palatine Hill, but which also has restrooms. There were two large ancient temples on the Palatine Hill, the Temple of Magna Mater (or Cybele, the Great Mother, on the high platform above the Iron-Age huts), and the temple of Heliogabalus, the result of a brief attempt of the emperor Elagabalus (reigned 218–222 CE) to shift the focus of Roman religion toward the Egyptian sun-god.

Garden on the Palatine Hill

THE IMPERIAL FORA

Beginning with Julius Caesar, and continuing with several of the early emperors, it became desirable to expand the forum beyond its original boundaries by buying up the surrounding land and creating adjunct fora (the word *fora* is the correct plural of *forum*). In reality, this was an attempt to control political power by shifting it away from the republican

The Ruins of a Fallen Empire

forum into a new space dedicated to the god or gods of an emperor's own choosing, often as a way of connecting the emperor's family with those gods, and certainly to make himself central in the minds of the people. Today, the imperial fora (the fora of the emperors) are along the main road called the Via dei Fori Imperiali, but in reality that street was built over large parts of the imperial fora, and so now we can only see a portion of them. The Via dei Fori Imperiali was built by the fascists of the early twentieth century to be Mussolini's own "Via Sacra"—the road where his parades would take place. Note that in front of each imperial forum is a statue of the emperor who built it.

The Forum of Caesar

Julius Caesar was not technically an emperor. He would have been, had he not been assassinated, but the first true emperor was his nephew Octavian, also known as Augustus. However, Julius Caesar did rebuild much of the republican forum, as well as expand the forum at its northwest corner. He used the spoils of the Gallic wars to buy the land behind the *curia* (on the same side of the Via dei Fori Imperiali as the main forum, but best seen from the street side). The three standing columns are from the Temple of Venus Genetrix (restored during the reign of Trajan, 98–117 CE). Caesar had dedicated the temple to Venus to perpetuate the myth that he was a descendant of the goddess. His intention in rebuilding the *curia* was to reorient it to be the connection between the old forum and his own forum, but to be controlled by him. In doing so, he destroyed the *comitia*, the ancient site where the people of the republic used to gather to vote, implicitly making the statement that the government would no longer hear the voice of the people. In his forum, he allowed only government functions and cultic rites but no commerce. Before the senate could move into their new *curia*, Caesar was assassinated in 44 BCE, in the senate's temporary meeting place in the portico of the Theater of Pompey. The Forum of Caesar was completed by Augustus, and embellished by future emperors.

The Forum of Peace/Vespasian

Across the street from the republican forum and the Forum of Caesar are the remains of the other imperial fora. The so-called Forum of Peace is actually the Forum of Vespasian, built after the war in Judea with money

Rome

from the spoils of Jerusalem. Though it was built in the early 70s, the name Forum of Peace is actually a reference to the end of the civil war that resulted from the death of Nero in 68 CE. In the year of 68–69 CE, there were four different emperors, and stability was not restored to the empire until Vespasian left the war in Judea to return to Rome and become emperor in 69 CE. However, that left his son Titus in charge of the siege of Jerusalem, and when Jerusalem fell, the temple was destroyed—according to some accounts, against his father Vespasian's wishes. The Forum of Peace is now mostly under the street, especially the intersection of the major streets Via dei Fori Imperiali and Via Cavour. Note the remains of the medieval Torre dei Conti (tower of the Conti family) built by Pope Innocent III (who was a Conti). The tower is built on the foundations of one of the corners of the Temple of Peace in the Forum of Peace (now it is on the northwest corner of the intersection). The existence of the tower is witness to a time when the powerful families of medieval Rome felt the need for fortresses within the city, but for our purposes, it helps to see the outline of the Forum of Peace. The opposite corner of the Forum of Peace is under the church of Santi Cosma e Damiano, and indeed the church itself was built into part of the remains of the forum, possibly the library or the office of the Urban Prefect. It is said that at one time, the Forum of Peace would have held the treasures taken from the Jerusalem temple.

The Forum of Nerva

Moving west along the Via dei Fori Imperiali, we come to the remains of the Forum of Nerva, also called the *Forum Transitorum* because it was meant to connect the Forum of Peace and the Forum of Augustus to the main forum. Therefore, it was narrow between the Forum of Augustus and the Forum of Peace, but long, reaching to the back of the Basilica Aemilia. This forum was begun by Domitian (reigned 81–96), and finished and dedicated in the year 97, by his successor Nerva (reigned 96–98). It was during the reign of Domitian that the apostle John was exiled to the island of Patmos, where he would write the book of Revelation, in the year 95. When Nerva became emperor, the persecution subsided, and John was apparently able to return to Ephesus. In the Middle Ages, the Forum of Nerva became a thoroughfare leading to the main forum (it is possible that the name *transitorum* comes from this time), and a few of the wealthier families built homes along the edges of what became a main road. Not much of this forum is visible today, since most of it is under the street.

The Ruins of a Fallen Empire

The Temple of Mars, in the Forum of Augustus

The Forum of Augustus

Augustus succeeded his uncle Julius Caesar to become the first true emperor, though opinions vary as to whether we should date his rule from the end of the civil war that ensued in the aftermath of Caesar's death (this would be 31 BCE, when Marc Antony and Cleopatra were defeated at the Battle of Actium), or from the time when he was given power by the senate and received the name *Augustus* (in 29 BCE). In any case, he ruled until the year 14 CE. After completing the Forum of Caesar, he built his own forum including the Temple of Mars Ultor, which was dedicated in 2 BCE, the year that Augustus was proclaimed *Pater Patriae* (father of the country). The dedication to Mars had a twofold significance. It was meant to honor the god of war for Augustus' victory over Caesar's killers. It was also meant to connect Augustus himself to the gods since Mars was supposed to be the father of Romulus, and since Augustus claimed descent from Romulus he was therefore also claiming to be a descendant of the gods. Statues around the perimeter of the forum depicted the genealogy of Augustus from the gods through the heroes of Rome's mythology. Augustus himself was depicted in some statues wearing the hood of the Roman priests. An example of one such statue of Augustus can be seen in the National Museum at the Baths of Diocletian. The hood was meant to shield the priest from seeing bad omens, should he look up into the sky at the wrong moment (apparently it was believed that if one did not see the bad omen, it didn't count). Since Augustus had to buy the land, his forum was not as large as he would have liked, but he refused to force people to sell their property. Thus the forum backs up against the *suburra*, an ancient residential area of Rome. The architecture is a modified Greek style, to show Augustus' belief that Rome was to be a rebirth of the golden age of Greece. In building the forum, Augustus used colored marble from all over the world to signify Rome's triumph over (and colonization of) its enemies. The Forum of Augustus became the new center of government for the empire. Governors of the provinces were commissioned and sent out from here. The young men of the aristocracy received the toga of manhood here. Victorious generals dedicated their victory crowns to Mars, and the trophies of war were displayed here. The early emperors held court here. In the middle ages a monastery was built over the site of the Temple of Mars, though nothing of it remains.

The Forum and Markets of Trajan

The Forum of Trajan

The Ruins of a Fallen Empire

With the emperor Trajan (reigned 98–117), the greatest of the imperial fora took the concept beyond simply a political and religious center to the ancient world's version of a mall, paid for with the spoils of Trajan's Dacian wars. The Forum of Trajan was created by digging out the earth from between what are now two hills. Note the Column of Trajan, which has an inscription that claims the dirt removed was once as high as the column (about 130 feet). The column has a spiral frieze that depicts all of Trajan's military exploits (some say it was once colorfully painted). Originally, the column had a statue of Trajan himself on top, though now Trajan has been replaced with St. Peter. The column was actually a huge

The Column of Trajan

gravestone, since it marked Trajan's mausoleum, and his ashes were placed in a golden urn in the base of the column. From the eleventh to the sixteenth centuries, the base of the column was consecrated as a church, though it would not really hold enough people to be an actual place of worship.

Rome

The Forum of Trajan was dedicated in 112 CE, with the column dedicated in 113. The forum eventually included a temple dedicated to the deified Trajan, finished by his successor Hadrian. The statues adorning the forum were not statues of the heroes of mythical Rome but of Trajan's contemporaries, which was a new concept at the time. The Basilica Ulpia was the main government and court building of Trajan's reign, and it contained the Ulpian library, one of the greatest libraries of the ancient world, in use until the fifth century. Most of the Forum of Trajan collapsed in an earthquake in 800 CE, after that it was scavenged for building materials to decorate later buildings and churches.

The Markets of Trajan at Night

Behind the Forum of Trajan are the Markets of Trajan, a six-story shopping mall, with 150 shops, pubs, and offices. Since shopping was

The Ruins of a Fallen Empire

considered a business transaction that required negotiation, it was usually done by men. However, women did shop for certain items (usually their own clothing and shoes) and the complex included *thermopoliae*, the Romans' version of a fast food take-out place. In the sixth century, the Markets of Trajan were occupied by the eastern army that came to Rome to liberate it from invading Goths. Today you can walk through the Markets of Trajan, which now includes a small museum of sculpture and architecture. The Markets of Trajan can be entered from around the corner on the Via IV Novembre (there is a staircase leading up from the parking lot adjacent to the northwest corner of the Forum of Trajan). While in the Markets of Trajan, look for the grooves in the thresholds of the shops. These were used for the wooden panels which closed the shops at night.

ROMAN TEMPLES AND OTHER MONUMENTS

The Pantheon

The Pantheon

As the name implies, the Pantheon is a temple originally dedicated to all the gods of ancient Rome. This does not necessarily mean that every one

33

of the traditional Greco-Roman gods was represented, simply that the emperor's favorite gods were collected in one place and meant to represent all the others. The original Pantheon was built by Marcus Agrippa (a different Agrippa from the ones mentioned in the New Testament). It was dedicated in 27 BCE, however it burned down (twice). The current temple was designed and built by the emperor Hadrian (reigned 117–138 CE) and was completed in about the year 126. The inscription says that Marcus Agrippa built it, but Hadrian had that put there as a tribute to the builder of the original. The architecture is unique—the dome was meant to represent the heavens, with niches around the circle for the important deities of Rome. A statue of the deified Julius Caesar occupied the place of honor in the main apse. The dome is a perfect half sphere, the diameter being exactly the same as the height from the floor. The dome is made of concrete, with progressively finer aggregate going upward, so that the concrete itself gets lighter as it goes higher up. This, along with the fact that there is no weight in the center of the dome due to the oculus, allows the dome to be suspended over such a great open space without supports other than what is in the walls.

The *oculus* (or, "eye," the hole in the middle of the dome) is almost thirty feet across, and acts as a spotlight shining on the niches that once held statues of the gods. The sunlight coming in through the oculus acted as both a calendar and a clock. The position of the light would have marked the solstices and equinoxes, and would shine on the entrance every day at noon. The huge bronze doors are original from the time of Hadrian, as are the columns which were taken at that time from the Baths of Nero (which is why the columns are not all the same). The outside of the dome was once covered with gilded bronze tiles, but these were removed in the early seventh century when the eastern emperor Phocas visited Rome. The Column of Phocas in the Roman Forum commemorated this imperial visit. He gave the Pantheon to the pope to be turned into a church, but he took the gilded bronze tiles to be sent back to Constantinople (the ship never made it there, it was intercepted by pirates). Thus, in 609 CE, the Pantheon became the Church of Santa Maria ad Martyres (St. Mary of the Martyrs). The remains of many unnamed martyrs were brought to the Pantheon and are now under the main altar. This was to commemorate All Saints Day, which at that time was celebrated in May.

In the eighth century, Pope Gregory III had lead installed on the outside of the dome to replace the bronze tiles and protect it. Later massive bronze beams from the portico were removed and melted down to

The Ruins of a Fallen Empire

make Bernini's *Baldacchino* (altar canopy) for St. Peter's Basilica, as well as the cannons for Castel Sant' Angelo. Pope Urban VIII, who had the beams removed, tried to make up for it by commissioning Bernini to add twin bell towers to the Pantheon. They were generally considered aesthetically repulsive and were removed in the nineteenth century, though one can still see them on older drawings of the Pantheon. Urban VIII, who was of the Barberini family, left his fingerprints on Rome to such an extent that it prompted the famous expression, *Quod non fecerunt barbari, fecerunt Barberini* ("What the barbarians didn't do, the Barberini

---

Gian Lorenzo Bernini (1598–1680)

Although this is not a book about art history, there are a few artists one should know in order to fully appreciate Rome. I will include them as we come to them. The first is Gian Lorenzo Bernini. Bernini was the greatest sculptor of the Baroque era (roughly 1600–1750), which is the era after the Renaissance (roughly 1450–1600). This makes Bernini the successor to Michelangelo in the line of great sculptors. In fact, Bernini had Michelangelo's talent for making stone look like flowing fabric. His most famous sculpture is probably the *Ecstasy of St. Teresa* (1646), which is in the church of Santa Maria della Vittoria. Another is similar to it, the *Blessed Ludovica Albertoni* (1668), in the church of San Francesco a Ripa. These two sculptures were criticized at the time because some felt that Bernini had made spiritual ecstasy look too erotic. In fact, the *Ecstasy of St. Teresa* is placed high up on the wall of the church so that it's difficult to see the look of rapture on Teresa's face.

Important works of Bernini in Rome:
Ecstasy of St. Teresa—Santa Maria della Vittoria
Blessed Ludovica Albertoni—San Francesco a Ripa
The Four Rivers Fountain—Piazza Navona
Altar (design)—Sant' Agostino
Angel Statues—Ponte Sant' Angelo
Piazza San Pietro—St. Peter's, Vatican
Fountain in Piazza San Pietro (left side facing the basilica)—St. Peter's, Vatican
Baldacchino—St. Peter's, Vatican
Bronze sculpture, *The Throne of Peter*—St. Peter's, Vatican
Statue of Longinus—St. Peter's, Vatican
Statue of Constantine—Portico of St. Peter's Basilica (far right in an atrium)
Fountain of the *Barcaccia* (little sunken boat)—Piazza di Spagna/Spanish Steps
Fountain of the Triton—Piazza Barberini
Statue of *Santa Bibiana*—Santa Bibiana
Large Statue of *Pope Urban VIII* (done with his students)—Capitoline Museum
Head of Medusa—Capitoline Museum
Elephant (designed but not completed by Bernini)—Santa Maria Sopra Minerva
Façade of Santa Maria del Popolo—Piazza del Popolo
Bust of Jesus (possibly his last work)—San Sebastiano

did"). Whenever you see bees depicted in a crest or on some work of art, that is the sign of the Barberini.

Today the Pantheon houses the tombs of the kings of Italy, as well as the tomb of the painter Raphael. Look for the tomb of Queen Margherita of Savoy, who is buried with her husband King Umberto I. Queen Margherita was the inspiration for the name of Pizza Margherita. Note that the design of the Jefferson Memorial in Washington D.C. was inspired by the Pantheon.

The Pantheon, Interior

Castel Sant' Angelo

The name Castel Sant' Angelo means "Castle of the Holy Angel." On the top there is a statue of an angel sheathing a sword (note that the angel is not drawing the sword, but putting it away). According to tradition, in the year 590 CE, Pope Gregory I (the Great) asked the people of Rome to pray for release from a plague. After a procession through the streets of Rome, Gregory saw a vision of an angel sheathing a sword, which was taken to signify that the plague would end, which it did.

The Ruins of a Fallen Empire

Castel Sant' Angelo (Mausoleum of Hadrian)

When you look at the castle today, you see a fortress with an inner circular core, and an outer battlement. Originally, this was the mausoleum of the emperor Hadrian (died 138 CE), and was only the central circle, probably with a statue of the emperor in a chariot on the top, much like a triumphal arch. It once held the ashes of Hadrian, as well as the next five emperors. However, in the Middle Ages, it became a fortress, changing hands several times among the powerful medieval families. In the fourteenth century, during the time when there were two rival popes, it became a papal castle and hideout for the legitimate Roman Pope Boniface IX. Fortifications and a papal apartment were added in the fifteenth century, along with the *Passetto*, or as my students like to call it, the "Pape Escape," a walled corridor leading from the Vatican to the castle. Pope Alexander VI (Borgia) had the Passetto and the walls rebuilt around the turn of the sixteenth century. The Passetto came in handy in 1527 when the pope had to flee the Vatican to the castle as German Lutherans (under orders from Charles V) invaded Rome. The pope had to stay in the castle for a month. Later in the sixteenth century, Pope Paul III renovated the papal apartment in the castle, and these rooms can be visited today. The battlements were added in the seventeenth century. The statue of the angel sheathing his sword on the top was added in the eighteenth century.

Rome

The castle once functioned as the treasury and archives of the Vatican. In one of the small rooms there is still a huge treasure chest, though it's now empty, because the Vatican treasury was raided by Napoleon in 1797. There is an entrance fee to get into the castle, but it is worth the visit, and in fact has a nice café with beautiful views of the city. You can walk around the battlements, get a good view of the "Pape Escape," and also climb to the top level for even more spectacular views.

Battlements of the Castel Sant' Angelo, with the Passetto

The Temples of the Largo Argentina and the Roman Theaters

The word, *largo* simply means a widened place in the road, and this is literally an archaeological site in the middle of the intersection of several major roads. There are four temples, cleverly labeled (from right to left as you're looking toward the west) Temples, A, B, C, and D. Temple A is the one on the far right. Note that the small roof and altar are medieval, since like many Roman ruins this was consecrated as a church in the Middle Ages. Temple D is mostly under the road to your left. We don't know much about these temples, except that they date from the fourth to the second centuries BCE. The reason they are worth mentioning here is that the structure behind the temples, you can just see it under the street, is the back of the Theater of Pompey. During the time that Julius Caesar was building his new *curia*, the senate was meeting in the portico of the Theater of Pompey, and it was here that Julius Caesar was assassinated on the Ides (15th) of March in the year 44 BCE.

The Theater of Pompey was built in the middle of the first century BCE, by Pompey the Great, the Roman general who conquered Palestine and turned Judea into a client kingdom under the umbrella of the Roman Empire. This was one of the first permanent theaters in Rome (the other is the Theater of Marcellus, near the river). Before these theaters were built, temporary bleachers were put up for special occasions, and taken down after the games or shows (which were always accompanied by pagan religious rituals). Greek theaters were built into a hill, but the Roman theaters were built up so that no hill was needed. The original theaters were a semicircle, but if you imagine putting two theaters together, completing the circle, you get an *amphitheater*, like the Colosseum.

The Theater of Marcellus was begun by Julius Caesar, to compete with the theater of his rival Pompey. It was completed by Augustus after Caesar's death, but Augustus dedicated it to Marcellus, his nephew and first choice for heir who had died in 23 BCE. Note that the Theater of Marcellus has a renaissance palace built into the top of it. Both theaters held over 10,000 people.

Temples B and A of the Largo Argentina

The Temples of the Forum Boarium

The Forum Boarium is the area at the base of the Aventine hill, at the bend in the River Tiber, just south of the Theater of Marcellus and the Tiber Island. It is traditionally said to be an old cattle market, though there is no direct evidence of this. In ancient times this was the first port of Rome and the departure point for the ferry across the river. The first bridges were built here, and one can still see the remains of the "Ponte Rotto," the broken bridge next to the Ponte Palatino. This may have been the site of the first "forum" or public square of Rome, and in fact the first gladiatorial games were held here as part of a funeral ceremony in 264 BCE. During the time of the empire, it became a kind of swampy slum, home to those on the lowest rungs of the social ladder. Facing the church of Santa Maria in Cosmedin, between the church and the river, are two ancient temples.

The round temple is the Temple of Hercules Victor. It's one of only a few round temples in Rome (the others are the temples of Vesta and Romulus in the forum and Temple B in Largo Argentina), which led some to speculate that this was a temple dedicated to Vesta. In some older books or maps you will still see it labeled as such. There was a legend that Hercules stopped here on his travels and killed a giant. The temple was built to commemorate this in the second century BCE, probably by Greek transplants who brought their dedication to Hercules with them from Greece. The statue of Hercules that is probably from this temple is now in the Capitoline Museum. This temple was eventually made into a church, called Santa Maria del Sole, but it is no longer in service as a church. The roof that you see today is not original, but was part of a reconstruction that included major parts of the structure.

The rectangular temple just to the north is the Temple of Portuna (sometimes Portunus, also called the Temple of Fortuna, or Fortune). Portuna was a goddess who was thought to watch over ports, and as we have seen this was the area of Rome's first port. Boats coming up the river could land here, making the Forum Boarium ideal for early trade. Some Romans believed that the goddess Portuna could make women more beautiful in the eyes of men by concealing their imperfections. This temple was also built in the second century BCE, and was also later converted into a church. In the eighth century CE, it temporarily became the Church of Santa Maria Aegyptarca (St. Mary in Egypt).

The Ruins of a Fallen Empire

The Temple of Hercules Victor in the Forum Boarium

The Roman Baths

Roman bath complexes were huge structures that would later be the inspiration for the great train stations of Europe and the U.S. They included a series of three bathing pools: hot, warm, and cold (like a swimming pool), as well as what might be the equivalent of a full service health club or country club, complete with libraries, lecture halls, and a gymnasium. Several of the most prominent emperors built their baths, which were open to the public (though men and women used them at different times). It is said that they could hold thousands of people at a time. One has to imagine that every wall was faced with marble, and the floors were covered with mosaics.

The Baths of Caracalla are the most intact, and one can walk through the complex and see the outline of the rooms, and even the mosaic floors of the pools. The emperor Caracalla (reigned 211–217) built the baths during his short reign in the early third century, but the grandeur of the baths outlived him, and in fact the complex was in operation until the sixth century. If you choose to visit the Baths of Caracalla, keep in mind as you walk around that Caracalla was the son of Septimius Severus, the one who murdered his brother Geta so that he could rule alone and ordered that Geta's name be chiseled off the Arch of Severus. Caracalla was also the emperor who granted Roman citizenship to all inhabitants of the empire, not only increasing their tax burden, but setting the stage for tests of loyalty that would result in increased persecution of Christians.

The Church of Santa Maria degli Angeli, Built into the Baths of Diocletian

The Baths of Diocletian were built by the emperor who reigned at the beginning of the Great Persecution, the worst (and last) persecution of the church by the Roman Empire. The bath complex was dedicated in about 305 CE, right at the time that Diocletian retired, leaving the empire in the hands of his ruthless son-in-law Galerius. According to tradition, Christians were forced to work on the baths, and many died during construction. The remains of these martyrs are said to be in the church of Santa Maria degli Angeli (St. Mary of the Angels) now on the site. In 1561, Michelangelo designed the Piazza della Republica and Santa Maria degli Angeli to be built on the foundations of the Baths of Diocletian. Note how the piazza follows the curve of the foundation of the bath complex, and the little church of San Bernardo (opposite Santa Maria degli Angeli) is round because it is built into the remains of part of the atrium of the baths. Eight of the massive columns within the church of Santa Maria degli Angeli are original from the baths, however the floor of the baths is six feet below the current floor of the church, so that the columns actually continue on beneath the floor—look for the false column bases with seams in them so they could be attached at the floor level. Eventually, other parts of the baths became a monastery, as well as the National Museum at the Baths of Diocletian (the "Therme," see below under *Museums*).

> **Michelangelo Buonarroti** (1475–1564)
> Michelangelo is well known as the most important artist of the Renaissance. He was an architect and a painter, but his first love was sculpting, and when he was commissioned to paint the Sistine Chapel, he begrudgingly put down his chisel for five years. Although he is also known for his works that are in Florence (the statue of *David*, and his painting of the Holy Family), his fingerprints are all over the city of Rome. Even more impressive than the *David* is his *Pietá*, the statue of Mary holding the dead body of Jesus. Michelangelo sculpted this masterpiece when he was only twenty-five years old. It is also unique in that it has his signature on the sash of Mary's dress. In addition to the church of Santa Maria degli Angeli, Michelangelo designed the dome of St. Peter's basilica, as well as the Piazza del Campidoglio on the Capitoline Hill. This latter project included the façades of the three buildings, including the double staircase leading up to the Palazzo Senatorio (Rome's city hall), the pedestal for the equestrian statue of Marcus Aurelius, as well as the ramp leading up to the square (it was originally longer but was shortened when the Via del Teatro di Marcello was put in), and the geometric design of the piazza, which was meant to draw it all together. Michelangelo was also the architect of a gate in the city wall known as the Porta Pia, on the northeast side of Rome. (This was the gate through which Italian troops entered Rome on September 20, 1870, resulting in the final unification of Italy. The street that begins at that gate and enters the city is now called, *Via XX Settembre*, or "September 20th Street").
>
> Important Works of Michelangelo in Rome:
> *The Pietá*—St. Peter's, Vatican
> Dome of St. Peter's Basilica—St. Peter's, Vatican
> *The Statue of Moses*—San Pietro in Vincoli
> *Statue of the Risen Christ*—Santa Maria Sopra Minerva
> Piazza del Campidoglio—Capitoline Hill
> The Church of Santa Maria degli Angeli—Baths of Diocletian
> Cycle of Old Testament Scenes—Sistine Chapel Ceiling
> *The Last Judgment*—Sistine Chapel Altar Wall
> Chapel of Leo X—Castel Sant' Angelo
> Porta Pia—Via Nomentana and Via XX Settembre

Rome

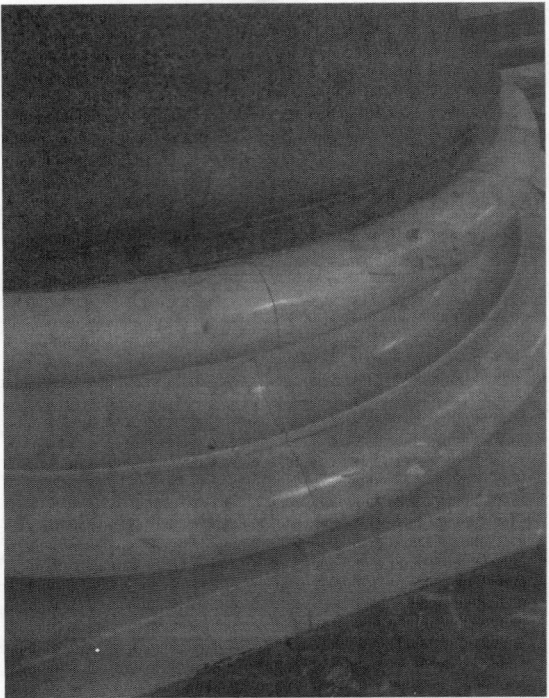

False Column Base in the Church of Santa Maria degli Angeli

At the time Santa Maria degli Angeli was being built, Michelangelo was already working on St. Peter's Basilica in the Vatican, and in fact many of the original paintings from the old St. Peter's are now in Santa Maria degli Angeli (the ones in St. Peter's today are mosaic copies of the original paintings). What is now the transept of Santa Maria degli Angeli was originally the *frigidarium* (cold pool) of the baths. This was originally meant to be the main nave of the church, but the orientation of the church was changed in a renovation of the eighteenth century by the architect Vanvitelli. One can see that this is the largest open space in the church, and it is obvious that this should be the main part of the church, however now the church is oriented so that the main altar is directly to the back from the entrance. An interesting curiosity to note is the meridian line, placed into the floor so that a beam of light from the sun crosses the line at approximately noon ("true noon") every day (though this may be closer to 1:00 p.m. local time due to daylight savings time).

The Ruins of a Fallen Empire

Interior of Santa Maria degli Angeli (Baths of Diocletian)

THE MUSEUMS

It would be impossible for any non-native to visit all of the museums of Rome. I list here the most important for the Christian pilgrim and student of early Christianity. Other museums, such as the Borghese Gallery in the Villa Borghese, are certainly worth a visit, especially for their treasures of Renaissance art, however they do not contain much that will enhance the spiritual nature of your pilgrimage. Note that when you enter some museums, you will be expected to check any large bags or backpacks in a locker. It's best to carry only a small bag with you on your daily tours of Rome, then you can keep your valuables with you (though I have never had any trouble leaving valuables with the museum guards).

Rome

The Piazza del Campidoglio, on the Capitoline Hill

The Capitoline Museums

The Capitoline Hill was once a center of Roman religion, since it was the site of the most important temple of ancient Rome, the Temple of Jupiter Optimus Maximus. This huge temple once occupied almost the entire top of the hill, Rome's "acropolis." Later, the Capitoline Hill became the center of government for the city of Rome, giving us our English word, "capital." In fact, the middle of the three large buildings that surround the piazza is the Palazzo Senatorio, still the seat of city government, and the office of the mayor of Rome. The piazza is called the *Piazza del Campidoglio*, and it was designed by Michelangelo, who brought the equestrian statue of Marcus Aurelius from its original site at St. John Lateran (the statue in the piazza is a copy of the original, which is inside the museum). The two buildings on either side of "city hall" are the Capitoline Museums, open to the public since the year 1734. If you're facing the Palazzo Senatorio, the building to your right (with the entrance to the museums) is the *Palazzo dei Conservatori* (we'll call it building 1) and the one to your left is *Palazzo Nuovo* (building 2). The two buildings are connected by a tunnel under the piazza, so you will enter building 1 and exit from building 2.

The Ruins of a Fallen Empire

As you enter the museum, you will first come into a courtyard, where you will find parts of the colossal statue of the emperor Constantine from the Basilica of Maxentius/Constantine in the forum. The reason that only the head, hands, and feet remain is because this was a composite statue—the parts that would represent exposed skin were in marble, but the rest of the statue was probably made of plastered wood or some other material that did not stand the test of time.

From the courtyard, go up to the main floor of building 1. Unless you have a lot of time, skip the top floor, since it only has paintings of minor significance, and you will easily use up a lot of time looking at room after room of them. Rather, go up to the main floor that contains the atrium (or *exedra*). Look for the larger-than-life statue of Mars. Parts of the statue are due to modern restorations (since it was found in pieces) but this may be the statue that would have been in the Temple of Mars Ultor in the Forum of Augustus. As you go through the halls of building 1, look for the room with the ancient statue of the "She-Wolf," a statue that may date back to the fifth century BCE, though the twins were added later, probably as recently as the fifteenth century. The room itself is decorated with the Roman *Fasti*, lists of the Roman consuls and victorious generals during the time of the Republic. When Michelangelo designed the Piazza del Campidoglio, he had these removed from the forum and placed as decoration in the piazza. They were, of course, later brought inside to protect them from the elements. Also look for Bernini's sculpture of the head of Medusa, and a statue of the emperor Commodus dressed as Hercules (wearing a lion skin).

In the atrium (*exedra*) is the equestrian statue of Marcus Aurelius (reigned 161–180). The one in the piazza is a copy of this original, which only escaped being melted down in the Middle Ages because they thought it was a statue of Constantine. Also in the atrium is the gilt bronze statue of Hercules from the Temple of Hercules in the Forum Boarium, as well as some fragments of another statue of Constantine. Finally, notice the remnant of the foundation of the Temple of Jupiter Optimus Maximus, which is still in its original place. What you see here is the foundation structure of the podium, or platform, on which the temple stood. The floor of the temple was actually higher than this. Built in the sixth century BCE, and rebuilt after a fire in the first century BCE, the temple was two hundred feet square. The main part of the temple was dedicated to Jupiter, the highest god of the Roman pantheon, with two side temples dedicated to the goddesses Juno and Minerva. The whole thing would have been capped off with a statue of Jupiter holding a bolt of lightning. During the time of the Republic, generals leaving for war would start from here, and victorious generals would end their triumphal parades here. Take a moment to touch the rough stones of volcanic rock—touch the sixth century BCE, and the Roman Republic. The early Roman Christians would have seen this large pagan temple set on the top of the hill.

Going back down the stairs, proceed down into the tunnel that connects the two buildings under the piazza. In the tunnel is a collection of ancient Roman grave markers, some of which have Christian symbols on them (see the list of Christian symbols below, in the section on the catacombs). Take some time to read the translations of the inscriptions. Where you see a Christian symbol, and if no one's looking, go ahead and touch the stones (you might get scolded by a guard if they see you do this, and I would *never* tell you to touch something that could be damaged, such as a painting, but if you're like me, touching the stones is an important part of feeling connected to the early Christians). Here you have the opportunity to touch something that was held by some of your ancestors in the faith, as they prepared their loved ones for burial. The people whose names are on these stones are part of that great cloud of witnesses who cheer you on as you travel the journey of the Christian life (Heb 12:1).

Before you leave the tunnel, go up the stairs in the middle of the tunnel that leads into the Tabularium. The Tabularium was the record hall of ancient Rome, built in the first century BCE, and restored by the emperor Claudius in 46 CE. Later, in the Middle Ages, the building was used as a warehouse for storing salt (you can still see residue from the salt on some of the walls). Much of what still stands was actually added in the fifteenth century, and there are some remains of various temples incorporated into the building. However, the most important thing not to be missed is the view of the forum from the balconies.

Proceeding on to building 2, there are two interesting rooms containing busts of emperors and philosophers. In the Hall of the Emperors, you can see portrait busts of each of the early emperors, though in the case of some, we are not really sure who the subject is, and the attribution of a certain emperor may come from a time when a private collector needed a bust of that emperor to complete his collection. It is interesting to note that before Hadrian, Roman men did not wear beards. Apparently, Hadrian had some facial feature he wanted to conceal (perhaps a scar), so he wore a beard, thus beginning a trend.

The National Museum at the Baths of Diocletian (Therme)

This museum is worth a visit, even if only for one thing: the colorfully painted walls of the first-century Roman houses, like the House of Livia on the Palatine Hill. These are frescos, painted in wet plaster, and they are still beautiful after two thousand years (so no touching here!). Several rooms have been reconstructed with the walls taken from excavations and set up so that you can walk into them. Take some time to stand in these rooms, and imagine what it would have been like to live in a house like this. No doubt only the wealthy had their walls painted like this, however keep in mind that while most Christians were not wealthy, many were slaves and might have lived or worked in places like this. Also note the detailed mosaic floors, and don't miss the pictures on the wall behind you showing the excavations and the mosaics in their original place.

There are some interesting statues in this museum, including a large statue of the emperor Augustus dressed as the Pontifex Maximus. Note the hood, which was worn to protect the priest from seeing any bad omens in the sky above him. There are also ancient coins and jewelry on the lower level.

The Vatican Museums and the Sistine Chapel

Contrary to what you might think, the Vatican Museums are not museums with exhibits *about* the Vatican, they are the Vatican's collection of antiquities and art. As such, there is actually not as much in here that is worth your time as you would think. Of course, everyone goes through the Vatican Museums because that's the only way to get to the famous Sistine Chapel, though it is sometimes sad to see the way people literally run past the Vatican collection just to get to the Sistine Chapel. There are a lot of exhibits in the Vatican Museums, some of which seem randomly organized, and no doubt there are different things that will be of interest to different people, from the many classical statues, to the Egyptian artifacts, to the tapestries, and on and on. I will only highlight what I think are the things not to be missed. If you limit your visit to these things, you can be in and out in a couple of hours, however to truly browse the seemingly endless halls, start early and plan to spend most of the day.

Rome

Sarcophagus Showing Jesus Raising Lazarus (Vatican Museum)

The most important thing for our purposes is the early Christian room. You will see this first, when you enter the museum, and you need to go to the right when everything else is to the left, or you'll miss it. Watch for the directional sign as you enter the museum. In the early Christian room you will probably experience a reprieve from the crowds since most people skip this. Take some time to look around at the early Christian grave markers and sarcophagi. Note the early Christian symbols (see below, under *Catacombs*). Look at the sculptures on the sarcophagi, and see if you can find depictions of biblical stories, such as the raising of Jairus' daughter, or the raising of Lazarus, all meant to convey a belief in resurrection and eternal life. Daniel's three friends in the furnace brought to mind the persecution. If you notice a carving of Jesus healing or raising someone, and it looks like Jesus is holding a "magic wand," you're not far off. Although no one actually thought Jesus used a wand, the wand symbolizes miraculous power, so that it doesn't look like Jesus is simply pointing at someone.

Sarcophagus Showing Daniel's Friends in the Furnace (Vatican Museum)

As you go through the halls of what once were the Papal Apartments, there are just a few things to highlight. Notice the giant porphyry (red marble) sarcophagi of the emperor Constantine. One was for his daughter Costanza, and was originally in her mausoleum, now the church of Santa Costanza. The other was probably meant for Constantine himself. In the Constantine Room, look for a mural of the Battle at the Milvian Bridge, which occurred on October 28, in the year 312. At this battle, Constantine defeated Maxentius to become the emperor of the Western empire, and Maxentius drowned in the Tiber. The mural is by a student of Raphael. In the Raphael Rooms, look for the famous painting, *School of Athens*. The two figures in the center are Plato (on the left) and Aristotle (on the right). Take a look at the background to see something like the way the Roman baths would have been decorated. Also in the Raphael Rooms, look for a painting of the meeting of Pope Leo the Great (bishop of Rome 440–461) with Attila the Hun. In about the year 451, Leo I of

Rome

Rome convinced Attila not to sack the city of Rome, which solidified the pope's position as protector of the city, in place of the imperial government. In the Fire Room (Sala del Incendio), look for the painting, *Fire in the Borgo*. This painting depicts a famous fire in the Borgo district, at the edge of the Vatican. In the background, you can see the façade of the old St. Peter's church, before it was demolished to build the present basilica.

At the end of the long and winding road that is the Vatican Museums, after what seems like an endless collection of modern art, you will finally come to the Sistine Chapel. You may find the Sistine Chapel a bit of a letdown. Yes, the paintings by Michelangelo are amazing, however, it is likely to be so crowded when you're in there that the combination of people talking, guards telling people to be quiet, and the pain in your neck from looking up will make the experience less than inspiring. Nevertheless, many people would say that you can't go to Rome and not see the Sistine Chapel. It's called the *Sistine* Chapel because it was originally commissioned by Pope Sixtus IV. It was designed to be the same dimensions as the biblical Temple of Solomon, roughly 132 feet by 44 feet. It was dedicated to the Virgin Mary of the Immaculate Conception on the feast of the Assumption in 1483. The paintings by Michelangelo were commissioned by Pope Julius II in 1508, and covered up the original ceiling, which was blue with painted stars (see the ceiling of Santa Maria Sopra Minerva for a good example of this older style). It took Michelangelo almost five years to complete the ceiling. Later, he came back and painted the altar wall with his famous *Last Judgment*, based on the writings of Dante. It was unveiled in 1541, and the demon with the donkey ears in the lower corner is actually a portrait of the pope's chamberlain who had criticized the work. In addition to the paintings by Michelangelo, note the paintings on the side walls, including works on the life of Moses by the renaissance master Botticelli, as well as the painting of Jesus giving the keys to Peter, by Pietro Perugino.

Chapter 3

Holy Ground

WHERE THE MARTYRS DIED

The Colosseum (Flavian Amphitheater)

Rome

The Colosseum

THE FIRST GLADIATORIAL CONTESTS were held as part of the funeral celebrations of ancient Roman kings, probably meant as a form of human sacrifice to bring divine favor on the departed king. Apparently, the gladiators fought to the death to see who would be the sacrifice. The "spectacles," as they were called, were originally held in the fora (since that's where the funeral ceremonies were held), first the Forum Boarium, and later the main Roman Forum. The first permanent theaters of Pompey and Marcellus inspired the *Flavian Amphitheater*, more commonly known as the Colosseum. The name "Colosseum" comes from the fact that the amphitheater was once next to the "colossus," a huge statue of the emperor Nero. So the name "colosseum" simply referred to the place, "at the colossus." But its true name is the Flavian Amphitheater, after the emperors of the Flavian dynasty who built it: Vespasian, Titus, and Domitian.

Construction on the Colosseum was begun by Vespasian in the year 69, not long after he became emperor, and it was probably meant as a gesture to appease the people of Rome by giving them back the land taken by Nero after the fire of 64. Most of the construction was ultimately paid for with the spoils of the war in Judea. The Colosseum was dedicated in 79 CE, but not really completed until 80, when it was rededicated by Titus with one hundred straight days of games, free and open to the public. This was one of the main ways that emperors and other important men of the empire would try to gain the approval of the people—*bread and circuses*, as it is said—meaning that the way to increase one's approval rating was to give the people food and sponsor entertainment. The people were happy to be entertained, and the shows and games of the amphitheater were extremely popular. The emperors did use the opportunity of the large gatherings in the Colosseum to distribute food and sometimes even hand out coins. For their part, the public felt free to express their opinions in the safety of numbers, and on occasion the emperor was even booed. The venue for public demonstration that was lost when the *comitia* was destroyed (by the Forum of Caesar) was transferred to the arena. Thus the amphitheater became both the "red carpet" of Roman high society and the voice of the people.

Spectators were given tokens with numbers indicating the gate they should enter and their seating section. One can still see the Roman numerals above the gates. Some of the seats were reserved, and archaeologists have found the names of later senators carved into a few of the seats. The Colosseum held about 50,000 people. It would have had a canvas canopy over the top, with a hole in the middle to let the sun shine on the arena. An elite corps of the Roman navy was assigned the duty of managing the ropes and riggings for the canopy, which could be adjusted to follow the movement of the sun so that the most important spectators remained in the shade. The emperor sat in a ringside box seat at the middle of the short axis of the oval, with the senators and Vestal Virgins around him. Other places of honor belonged to whomever happened to hold certain prestigious offices, and the rest of the seats were organized by decreasing social status as one moved up the bleachers, with the women in the nosebleed section.

The Colosseum held several different kinds of spectacles. A typical day of games might begin with hunts, in which scenery was set up and many different kinds of animals were brought in to be killed by the "hunters." Huge amounts of money was spent to import the most exotic animals that could be found, and so many of them were killed that a few species almost became extinct because of it. It is said that there were even occasions when the center arena was filled with water to reenact naval battles in small scale ships. However this probably only happened in the first year of operation, before Domitian added the underground tunnels.

Over the lunch hour there would be public executions, often of those sentenced to *damnatio ad bestias* (condemnation to the beasts). Those condemned to die in this way were sent into the arena to face the lions, or in fact any one of a number of animals, including leopards, elephants, bulls, boars, or even ostriches. Although the stories of Christians being thrown to the lions include some legendary material, there is no doubt that some Christians died in this way in the Colosseum. However, since the Colosseum was not built yet in the time of Nero, no Christians could have been martyred here during his persecution.

After an interlude of musical and/or dramatic performances, the afternoon was dedicated to the gladiators. Most of the gladiators were probably also condemned criminals who simply stayed alive as long as they kept winning. There were some men who voluntarily chose the life of a gladiator, perhaps as a way to escape overwhelming debt or to seek personal glory, however volunteering to be a gladiator was frowned upon by Roman society and any aristocratic man who signed up would thereby lose his social status. Still, for the best gladiators, winning could lead to rock-star-like fame and popularity. The best gladiators were called, *suspirium puellarum*, those who make the girls sigh. However, since the Colosseum was the Broadway of gladiatorial venues, the gladiators who made it this far were considered very valuable, so there were fewer fights to the death in this arena than one might think. It is true that the emperor Commodus did dress as a gladiator and fight in the arena, but his battles were all staged to make sure he would win.

The Colosseum (Flavian Amphitheater)

When looking at the Colosseum from the outside, notice the levels, each with its own order of columns. From the ground up the capitals of the columns progress through the architectural stages of ancient Greece: Doric (flat), Ionic (looks like a scroll), and Corinthian (ornate with sculptures of leaves and vines). Look for the Roman numerals above the gates that marked the seating sections. Also remember that although much of the higher parts have fallen down, the level of the tallest part of the Colosseum continued all the way around the circle.

The Colosseum was struck by lightning twice in the third century, and was repaired by the emperor Decius. It was damaged in the Gothic invasion in 410, and by three different earthquakes in the late fifth and early sixth centuries. It was repaired again, but the gladiator games were discontinued in the fifth century, and only the hunting shows continued into the sixth century. After yet another earthquake in the middle of the ninth century, it began to be picked over for materials for other buildings. The many holes you see in the stones once had iron clamps or pegs, but these were pulled out to be melted down to make cannonballs and other armaments in the Middle Ages. Eventually, poor squatters built shacks against the walls of the Colosseum, and used it as a pen for livestock. One of the powerful medieval families even tried to turn it into their personal fortress. It was not until 1675 that the Colosseum stopped being looted for building materials. In that year, Pope Clement X dedicated the Colosseum as holy ground because Christians had once been martyred here. His inscription says that the site had been, "cleansed of impure superstition by the blood of the martyrs." The brick supports that you see on the exterior were put up in the nineteenth century to prevent further collapse.

As you walk around the interior of the Colosseum, make sure to look out to the west, toward the Temple of Venus and Roma, the double temple that marks the eastern end of the Roman Forum. The temple facing the Colosseum was the Temple of Venus. The Temple of Roma faced the forum, though now its remains are built into the church and monastery of Santa Francesca Romana.

In the middle of the oval is the arena. You can see the underground tunnels built by Domitian for the movement of gladiators, animals, and scenery. There would have been a wooden floor over the tunnels, covered with sand to absorb the blood (in fact our English word *arena* is simply the Latin word for sand). The underground tunnels also led out of the Colosseum to the *Ludus Magnus*, the largest of four training grounds in

Remains of the Ludus Magnus, with the Colosseum in the Background

the area around the Colosseum. This one can still be seen partially excavated in an area below the street just to the east. From the end of the Via di San Giovanni in Laterano, you can see the oval of the small training arena (half under the street) surrounded by the remains of gladiators' barracks and armory storage rooms. This is where the gladiators trained, and here wealthy men with a lot of free time would watch the training and bet on the matches.

Near the Colosseum is the triumphal Arch of Constantine. Dedicated in the year 315, it is meant to commemorate a decade of rule. Even though Constantine did not actually become the emperor in the western empire until the year 312 (and 324 in the east), he was counting his reign from the time when he was proclaimed emperor by his father's legions. He had joined his father, the general Constantius, in Britain in the year 305, and the troops acknowledged him as the heir and the next emperor. Constantius died in 306, and the legions vowed their loyalty to Constantine. For all practical purposes, the arch celebrates the victory of the Battle at the Milvian Bridge, on October 28, 312. Most of the sculptures and ornamentation on the arch were taken from other monuments, such as in the Forum of Trajan, as a way to show that Constantine was now the emperor and successor to the great emperors of the past. In fact Hadrian's beard was chiseled off of his image to turn it into a portrait of Constantine. There are numerous depictions of water gods, which may have been deliberate to remind the viewer of Maxentius' death by drowning in the Tiber at the Milvian Bridge. There are a few sections of the sculptures that were created originally for this arch—they are primarily the thin rectangular friezes at the level of the arches, just below the large circular medallions. The one on the south side (the side facing away from the Colosseum) on the right hand side of the arch shows the Battle at the Milvian Bridge and the death of Maxentius. The main inscription on the arch says that it was dedicated by the Senate and People of Rome (SPQR) to Constantine, who, "by divine inspiration and greatness of mind" was the avenger of Rome against the tyrant Maxentius. The words, "divine inspiration" are probably a reference to Constantine's vision in which he heard the voice of God telling him to march into battle under the banner of Christ. Inscribed on the vault (underside) of the main arch are the words, *Liberatori Urbis—Fundatori Quietis* (To the liberator of the city, the founder of peace). The fact that Constantine was a flawed man and emperor notwithstanding, the juxtaposition of the Arch of Constantine next to the

Colosseum is a larger than life reminder that in the early fourth century, the church went from persecuted to privileged, almost overnight.

The Arch of Constantine

The Roman Circus

The Roman circus was actually a *hippodrome*, or a track for horse races. (The small oval in the gardens of the imperial palace on the Palatine Hill was once thought to be a circus, however it was probably at most only used for training horses, or perhaps for private gladiatorial contests.) A Roman circus was like an elongated oval with one flat side, and a *spina*, or central "spine" down the middle. The horses, usually pulling chariots, raced seven times around the track counterclockwise. The jockeys were organized into teams designated by colors: the red team, the blue team, the green team, and the white team. Just like modern sports loyalties, everyone had his favorite team. A fan could buy a mug with his team on it, and sometimes rival groups of fans broke out into riots. In the later empire, the four teams evolved into factions, something like political parties.

In addition to horse races, the track could be home to many other kinds of spectacles, including acrobats and animal acts—just the kinds of things we might expect to see at a modern circus. However these spectacles also included public executions, sometimes by crucifixion. During times of persecution, more Christians were martyred in the circuses than in the Colosseum. The most famous circus is, of course, the *Circus Maximus*, at the southern foot of the Palatine Hill. This was the largest, holding around 300,000 people in its bleachers. Originally, it had two Egyptian obelisks along the *spina*—they are now in the piazzas at San Giovanni in Laterano and Piazza del Popolo. The Circus Maximus was damaged in the fire of 64, and the emperor Nero had to have it rebuilt. It continued to be used for races until the sixth century.

The *Circus of Nero* was built as an alternative to the Circus Maximus. However, Nero's circus was outside the city walls, on a hill already known as the Vatican Hill. After the great fire of 64, a fire that Nero himself probably started to make room for a new palace, the Christians were blamed for the fire and became the scapegoats for all the ills of Roman society. We have noted that the Colosseum was not built yet, so no Christians could have died there during Nero's persecution. Christians martyred under Nero would have died in the Circus of Nero, and this included the apostle Peter, who probably died in 65 (though some say as late as 67). According to tradition, Peter was crucified upside down, because he believed he was not worthy to die in the same manner as his Lord, and he begged his captors to execute him another way. They mockingly complied, hanging him upside down. Because Nero's circus was outside the city walls, there was a *necropolis* (literally, "city of the dead"), or cemetery, very close by. Peter was buried in a grave along the north side of the circus, in a spot that is still to this day directly under the main altar of St. Peter's Basilica in the Vatican.

One of the most popular gathering spaces in Rome is Piazza Navona, built on the foundations of the *Circus of Domitian*. One can clearly see the outline of the circus in the shape of the square (which is not square) and especially in the semi-circular buildings at the north end. The emperor Domitian built this in 86 to be his stadium, and it is said that the arena could be filled with water to make a public swimming pool in the hottest part of the summer. Whenever the Colosseum was out of commission due to fire or earthquake, the gladiator contests were moved

Holy Ground

here. One can assume that during the persecution of Domitian (when the apostle John was exiled to the Island of Patmos), Christians in Rome were martyred here. The festive (one might say circus-like) atmosphere of the present piazza might tempt us to forget that this is holy ground. Note that one can still see parts of the bleacher supports under the buildings at the north end. Some remains of the substructure can be seen from the outside of the piazza along the Via dei Coronati and Piazza Cinque Lune. There is also a door from inside Piazza Navona leading into one of the buildings at the top of the curve. If the door is open, you can go in past some offices and onto a small interior balcony where you can get a good look at the arches that held the bleachers. Under these arches, the prostitutes would loiter, hoping to entice customers coming from the shows. At the center of Piazza Navona is Bernini's fountain of the *Four Rivers*, completed in 1651. The four figures are the personifications of the four great rivers of the world as Bernini saw it: The Danube, the Ganges, the Nile, and the Rio de la Plata. They are supposed to represent the four corners of the earth, with Rome at its center. The obelisk on the fountain was originally from the Circus of Maxentius, outside the city on the Appian Way.

Piazza Navona (The Circus of Domitian)

Rome

WHERE THE MARTYRS WERE BURIED

Since there was a law against burials within the city walls, the cemeteries were all outside the walls, on the outskirts of the city. In some places, the volcanic rock (called *tufa*) was soft enough to dig but sturdy enough to support the weight of layers of tunnels. Before long, these areas were being used for burials, especially for the early Christians, since most pagan Romans were still being cremated until the third century. One particular site (the area now occupied by San Sebastiano) was called "the hollows" because it was near an area where *tufa* was quarried for building blocks. The underground cemetery there became referred to as the one "at the hollows," in Latin, *ad catacumba*. Eventually the term "catacombs" became the generic name for all of these underground burial chambers. Wealthy families began to make their underground mausoleums available to their Christian family, the church, and separate burial chambers were connected by tunnels, to create subterranean labyrinths extending for miles.

The tunnels were carved out by professional gravediggers called *fossors*. You can still see the marks from their picks in the walls and ceilings of the tunnels. The deceased were placed in niches called *loculi* (singular: *loculus*) that were cut into the tufa walls. Their bodies were wrapped in linen and possibly covered with plaster, like a full body cast. The loculus was then covered with tiles and the name of the beloved departed was painted on the tiles in red paint. If the family was not literate, or if they worried about not finding their way back to the right loculus, they might imbed a small shell, or personal item (or even a small toy if the grave was that of a child) in the plaster to mark the spot. If the family was wealthier, the loculus might be covered with a marble slab inscribed with the person's name. Some families were wealthy enough to afford a family tomb, called a *cubiculus*, which was basically a small room with niches surrounding a central larger niche that held a sarcophagus. The sarcophagus probably was meant to hold multiple bodies, and was placed under an arch called an *arcosolium*, because the arc of the arch was symbolic of the sun's apparent movement across the sky.

When Christians were executed for their faith during times of persecution, they came to be called *martyrs*, which is the Greek word for "witnesses." The martyrs were buried in the catacombs, but often their tombs were designated as places of special reverence and embellished with inscriptions. Sometimes only parts of the martyrs' bodies could be recovered from the arenas, so that a small loculus could be that of a child, or it may be the remains of a martyr who had been burned or left unburied for some time. It became desirable for other Christians to be buried as close to the martyrs as possible, since it was felt that the martyrs were close to God, so the catacombs began to grow around the tombs of the martyrs. Sometimes a chapel was built into the catacomb around a martyr's tomb. After the persecutions, if the tomb became a popular pilgrim site, it was decorated even more and additional staircases were built to accommodate the pilgrims and help them find the site more easily. However this made it increasingly difficult for later Christians to be buried near the martyrs.

Inside the Catacombs

Contrary to popular myth (perpetuated by the "sword and sandal" movies of the 1950s and 1960s), the catacombs were never used as a place to hide from the Roman authorities during times of persecution. Since they were all legally registered burial grounds, the Romans knew where they were. While not technically owned by the church, groups of Christians could have control over certain catacombs by organizing as funeral societies—Roman clubs meant to ensure proper burial for their members. We know that during the time that Zephyrinus was bishop of Rome

Rome

(199–217), his successor Callistus was a deacon and was in charge of managing the catacombs that now bear his name. Many Christians who died in the persecutions (including several bishops of Rome) were buried in the catacombs of Callistus. However, worship services were generally not held in the catacombs during the time of persecution, with the possible exception of some funeral Masses and memorials of the martyrs, and there are a few chapels in the catacombs for this purpose. The myth probably comes from the fact that Sixtus II of Rome (bishop 257–258) was killed in the catacombs of San Callisto on August 6, 258 CE. He was probably presiding over a funeral Mass when (as bishop Cyprian of Carthage relates in a letter) he was found by Roman guards and murdered right there on the spot, along with four deacons. During the persecution of the emperor Valerian, in 257–258 CE, the emperor had issued an edict forbidding Christian assembly, especially in the catacombs, and had his guards watching the catacombs. This led to the creation of false entrances and secret entrances, but even then it would not have been wise for Christians to hide in the catacombs.

The earliest Christians had a tradition of a kind of potluck meal called the *agape*, or love feast. At the very beginning of the church's history, the Eucharist was done as part of that meal, following the example of Jesus at the Last Supper. The apostle Paul complained that the Christians of Corinth were disrespecting the meal and each other in 1 Corinthians, chapter 11. Probably for various reasons, including the potential for abuse, the difficulty of getting larger groups of Christians together at one time for a meal, and the pressure that persecution placed on Christian assembly, the sacrament of the Eucharist became separated from the meal. As we can see in Justin Martyr's *First Apology*, by the middle of the second century the sacrament of the Eucharist is the central feature of Sunday morning worship, but the meal is not part of the worship service. It is possible that in some places, the meal became an evening meal, perhaps on Sunday evenings, when the Christians in a certain place would regather to share dinner. Eventually, however, the *agape* came to be combined with the tradition of the *refrigerium*, or the memorial meal (as Jesus said, "Do this in memory of me"). The *refrigerium* was held to remember a departed loved one, at least annually on the anniversary of his or her death. It was quite literally a picnic, held as close to the gravesite as possible, sometimes above ground, but often in the catacombs. It is possible that in the family tombs, the top of the sarcophagus itself under the arcosolium became the table from which the food was served. Since those who died in Christ were considered more alive than ever, the day of their death came to considered the day that they were born to eternal life, a kind of eternal birthday. This day was then more important than their earthly birthday, and was celebrated as a kind of holiday or feast day. In the case of the martyrs, their feast days were celebrated with the reading of Scripture, the reading of the stories of the martyrs, and sometimes with Mass, where again, the lid of the sarcophagus itself might serve as the altar table.

Christians would visit the catacombs to pay their respects to the martyrs, to pray for the peace of the departed souls, and to ask for their intercession. Since it was assumed that martyrdom guaranteed salvation, the martyrs were the "saints for sure," the ones whom you could safely assume were with their Lord in heaven. This meant that they had the Lord's ear, and so if you could ask a Christian brother or sister here on earth to pray for you (Jas 5:13–16), why not a brother or sister in heaven, who was close to God and could intercede in person? The fact that the saints could hear one's prayers did not imply that they were omniscient, only that their resurrected state allowed them to know one's prayers as a gift related to their proximity to God. The desire for the martyrs' intercession is attested by many inscriptions, such as this one: *Ora pro nobis quia scimus te in Christum* (Pray for us, for we know that you are in Christ).

When the emperor Constantine built the first basilica churches in Rome, several of them were outside the city walls, at the sites of the catacombs. They were built so that the martyr's tomb would be directly under the altar (as in Revelation 6:9). In at least one case, *loculi* above the martyr's tomb were removed, and the church was built half buried in the ground so that the altar was right above the martyr's remains. In other instances, the martyr's remains were brought up to the surface, in a spot directly over where they were, creating a new crypt, or *confessio*, highly decorated to look like a stylized catacomb, complete with a tunnel that led around the back of the altar for pilgrims to visit the martyr's tomb. This is one reason for the canopy (also known as *baldacchino* or *ciborium*) over the altar—the altar itself is considered a tomb. Another reason for the canopy is a reference to John 1:14. In becoming human, the Word of God "pitched his tent" among us, as the Greek says. So the concepts of the incarnation and the mortality of humanity are connected at the altar. Sometimes sarcophagus lids were deliberately used in the construction of altar tables. Eventually, the relics of less popular or unknown martyrs would be brought to a church and placed inside the altar, making the altar into as much a coffin as a table.

The Church of Santi Nereo e Achilleo, in the Catacombs of Domitilla

The catacombs fell out of use when the barbarian invasions of the fifth and sixth centuries made them unsafe. However, pilgrimage to the catacombs continued long after the catacombs were no longer used for new burials. After the legalization of Christianity, the popes set aside money for the upkeep and restoration of the catacombs. The barbarian invasions had resulted in the desecration of some of the catacombs, so they had to be renovated, and in the process the tombs of some of the martyrs were decorated. Much of this was done by Pope Damasus (bishop of Rome 366–383), who even wrote poems to be placed as inscriptions at the martyrs' graves. Eventually, Sunday Mass was being celebrated in the catacombs, which continued until the seventh century. Pilgrims came with gifts of oil for the lamps, which burned continuously, and they hoped to bring something back home with them that would be a kind of spiritual souvenir of their pilgrimage. Some took a small amount of oil from the lamp that was burning at the tomb of their favorite saint. Others would touch the martyrs' grave with a handkerchief or some other personal item. Anything that had come into contact with the martyr's tomb became a reminder of the believer's pilgrimage, a kind of

Holy Ground

secondary relic, which was sometimes thought to have healing power. However, by the seventh or eighth century, grave robbing (some of it by people who wanted to steal the relics) became such a problem that the remains of the martyrs began to be transferred from the catacombs to the churches within the city walls. Pope Pascal I (bishop of Rome 817–824) was responsible for much of the movement of the relics, and many relics of unnamed martyrs ended up in churches such as Santa Prassede. This meant that to be buried near the martyrs, one now had to be buried in the churches, so that the space under the floors of the churches became the cemeteries for wealthier Christians, and for the leaders of the church. The end result of this was that the pilgrims now went to the churches rather than to the catacombs. The confessio often had a hole or small door in it, so that pilgrims could still touch the tomb with a handkerchief, or drop in coins or small votive offerings. The feasts of the saints that had once been held in the catacombs became part of the church's ministry to feed the poor.

The very location of many of the catacombs was eventually forgotten until they were rediscovered and explored in the early days of archaeology. There was a time when one could wander into a catacomb and explore with it with a torch, however, there are stories of people who went in to the miles and miles of tunnels and never came out. Thankfully today they are mapped and well lit, and though only parts of them are open to the public, they all have experienced guides who will make sure you don't get lost.

The earliest existing Christian art is in the catacombs. Some of it is simply graffiti left by the mourners or pilgrims, but there are also many important and beautiful paintings decorating the tombs of the martyrs. Common narrative themes that you will see are the biblical stories of Daniel's three friends in the furnace (symbolic of persecution), Jonah (the three days in the great fish are a metaphor for the three days from Jesus' passion to his resurrection), Noah in the ark (symbolizing God's rescue from danger, the ark is often stylized so that the image looks like a man standing in a box), and Jesus raising Lazarus from the dead (taken as a promise of resurrection for all Christians, the image usually looks like Jesus is calling a small mummy out of a phone booth). There are also many representations of baskets of bread with fish, which not only reminds the viewer of Jesus feeding the multitudes but also becomes a symbol of the Eucharist. Finally, you may notice depictions of baskets of scrolls (which may simply look like small circles in a cylinder). This represents the Scriptures and/or doctrinal orthodoxy. Note that biblical stories are not depicted as narratives, but rather as vignettes that are suggestive of the whole story. Therefore, the artists were not concerned about the details, but simply wanted to give the viewer a pictorial reminder, assuming the viewer already knew the story and its theological significance.

Grave Marker with Jesus Raising Lazarus (Vatican Museum)

In addition to the biblical stories, certain symbols appear with some frequency in the catacombs and on other Christian grave markers. Look for these:

- The **palm branch**, or **palm tree**, which could symbolize martyrdom and/or eternal life. However the palm branch as a symbol of the afterlife was not used exclusively by Christians. For the Romans it was a symbol of victory, so that in the Christian context it becomes a metaphor for the victory of life over death. The existence of a palm on a grave does not by itself prove that it was the grave of a Christian.

Holy Ground

- The **dove** and/or **olive branch**, which reminded the viewer of the story of Noah, and symbolized peace and rest. The dove would also have symbolized the Holy Spirit.

Grave Marker with Dove and Olive Branch (Vatican Museum)

- The **praying figure**, sometimes called the orant, from the Latin *orans*, which means, "praying." This a standing figure, with arms held up. This may be a holdover from pagan use, but when combined with other Christian symbols it may represent the deceased person, the soul in general, or a personification of the church. In these latter cases, the figure may appear to be a woman, even if the deceased was a man. We know that early Christians prayed in this position, sometimes even stretching the arms out to put themselves in the posture of Jesus on the cross.
- **Grape vines** or **grape leaves** (often they look like valentine hearts with stems). This comes from Jesus' words in John chapter 15, "I am the vine, you are the branches . . ." and represents unity with Christ and unity in the body of Christ. However, it may be that pagans also used this motif as a symbol of happiness (because of its association with wine), so it may be simply a symbol of the hope of a happy afterlife. Like the palm, this symbol by itself does not prove that a grave is Christian, but when used with other Christian symbols, it takes on its theological meaning.
- The **fish** is a well-known Christian symbol, often seen on the bumpers of cars. The symbol actually represents an acronym, in which a

Greek word for fish, *IChThYS*, spells out the first letters of the words, *Iesous Christos Theou Yios Soter*, or "Jesus Christ, God's Son, Savior." The fish symbol may originally have simply been meant as a reminder that Jesus said his disciples would fish for people, however by the third century, it also brought the full meaning of the acronym to mind.

Grave Marker with Fish and Anchor. Note the word Ichthys (in Greek: IXØYC) and the word Zwntwn, which means "living."(Vatican Museum)

- The Greek letters **Alpha and Omega**, a reference to Revelation 1:8; 21:6; and 22:13. Sometimes with a cross.
- The **ship**, which symbolized the church and reminded the viewer of Jesus calming the storm. The concept of a storm tossing the ship of the church might bring to mind the persecution.
- The **anchor**, which symbolized the church, the Christian faith, and the hope of eternal life as a safe harbor in which the ship of the church (or the soul) would find peace and rest.

Holy Ground

Grave Marker with Chi-Rho (Chi turned sideways to make a cross) with Alpha and Omega (Vatican Museums)

- The **dolphin**, which could symbolize resurrection and/or eternal life, though the dolphin was also used by some pagans who believed that dolphins carried the souls of the departed to the afterlife. Sometimes the dolphin was combined with the anchor, which would imply a specifically Christian use.
- The **peacock**, which was another symbol borrowed from pagan iconography and represented eternal life.
- What appears to be a large **asterisk** is meant to be a cross with the Greek letter *chi* superimposed over it. The *chi* is the first letter in *Christos*, or Christ, and looks like a capital X. A variation of this may not have the cross beam of the cross, it may be the Greek letter *iota*, or I, superimposed over the *chi*. In this case, it would be the initials of Jesus Christ (Jesus, spelled with an I, as in *Iesous*).
- The "**chi-rho**," which is the monogram of Christ. The letters *chi* and *rho* are the first two letters of *Christos* in Greek. The *chi* looks like an X, and the *rho* looks like a P superimposed over the X. Sometimes the X is turned sideways so that it also makes a cross. Note that this symbol was probably not used before the legalization of

Christianity. It is associated with the story of Constantine's vision, on the eve of the Battle at the Milvian Bridge in the year 312. It is said that Constantine saw the chi-rho emblazoned on the sky, accompanied by the words, *In hoc segno, vinces* (in this sign, you will conquer). Constantine then had the symbol placed on the standards of his legions, and marched into battle under the banner of Christ. He won that battle, on October 28, 312, which is now remembered as Milvian Bridge Day.

Grave Marker with Chi-Rho, Monogram of Christ, and Dove (Vatican Museum)

- The *Agnus Dei*, or Lamb of God, sometimes with an anchor or cross.
- You may also see some common abbreviations, such as the indications that the person buried in a particular tomb was a martyr. These include the capital **M** (the first letter of the word "martyr" in both Greek and Latin), or a combination of the first and last letters of the word "martyr," **MR** (for the Latin version) or **MP** (for the Greek).
- If the person was a bishop, one might see the abbreviation **EP**, for *Episcopos*, the Greek word for "overseer" or bishop.
- The abbreviation **IH** is the first two letters of the name of Jesus in Greek.

- The abbreviation **BM** stands for *bonae memoriae*, meaning, "of blessed memory."
- The abbreviation **DM** or **DOM** is actually a pagan inscription that continued to be used on Christian tombs. Originally it was a dedication, "to the departed spirits" (DM) or "to all the departed spirits" (DOM), but later it came to have the connotation of our "R.I.P." Some sources claim that DOM is an abbreviation for *Dominus* (Lord) making it a dedication to Christ, however that is not really true; it is just meant to give a Christian meaning to an embarrassingly long continued use of a pagan inscription.
- Finally, you may see abbreviations that indicate a high social class of the deceased. Those of the senatorial class might place **CV** (for *clarissimus vir* or "illustrious man") or **CF** (for *clarissimus foemina* or "illustrious woman") on the tombs of their loved ones. However, these tended not to be used by Christians, who believed that all members of the body of Christ are equal in God's eyes.

The Catacombs of Priscilla

The catacombs of Priscilla are not named for the Priscilla mentioned in the New Testament, as the church of Santa Prisca is sometimes said to be. Rather, inscriptions in the family tombs tell us that these catacombs were originally on land that belonged to the Acili family, and were started from their tombs. Priscilla must have been a member of that family. Some sources make her the wife of the senator Pudens, and therefore the mother (or grandmother) of Prassede and Pudenziana (see the churches of Santa Prassede and Santa Pudenziana below). In any case, the use of this catacomb probably goes back at least to the second century, and in spite of the fact that regular liturgy was not held here that early, its use for funeral and memorial Masses makes it the earliest known place of Christian worship. When you're in the catacombs of Priscilla, remember that you are standing on the same holy ground where your fellow Christians prayed only a few generations after Christ.

The catacombs of Priscilla contain the earliest painting of the Madonna and Child, probably from the second century. It also contains the so-called Greek Chapel, including ornate frescoes with colors still vivid after almost two thousand years. There is a phoenix painted in one of the scenes, though now it is difficult to see. This mythical bird was said to rise from its own ashes, and for some early Christians it was a symbol of resurrection. The Roman bishop Clement (88–97) in his letter to the Christians of Corinth (*1 Clement*) used the story of the phoenix as a literary device to talk about resurrection. Although it is rare as a Christian symbol, there are a few places in Rome where the phoenix appears. The phoenix is usually depicted as a small bird (often sitting in palm tree) with what look like rays of light coming from its head. Also look for a painting of a eucharistic scene, a depiction of the Good Shepherd, and an inscription with an anchor and two fish.

The Catacombs of San Sebastiano (and Pilgrim Church of San Sebastiano)

Saint Sebastian was a martyr of the Great Persecution, under the emperor Diocletian (reigned 284–305). Though he is often depicted as having been shot with arrows, there are few details about his martyrdom. According to an early legend Sebastian was a soldier in the praetorian guard, who was discovered to be a Christian because he was engaged in acts of charity for the church and the poor. He was sentenced to the firing squad (which at this time meant bows and arrows) and he was shot with multiple arrows, however like many martyr legends, the first attempt at killing him did not work. This is why he is usually depicted alive with his eyes open and looking up to the heavens (reminiscent of the martyrdom of Stephen in Acts 7:56–59), in spite of the many arrows stuck into his body. In any case, the legend goes on to say that his body was thrown into the sewer, but his clothing got caught on something, and rather than ending up downstream, his body hung there until a noble Christian woman named Lucina was told in a dream where to find him. He was then buried in the catacombs that are now named after him. Since his tomb was a popular pilgrim site, a church was built over the catacombs in the fourth century, however at first it was not named after Sebastian. The church of San Sebastiano was originally called the *Basilica Apostolorum*, or the Basilica of the Apostles, because of a tradition that the bodies of the apostles Peter and Paul were brought to these catacombs in the third century to protect them during a time of persecution. There are some unanswered questions about this, and the reliability of that tradition has been questioned by scholars, however Pope Damasus (366–383) placed an inscription here, which claims both Peter and Paul as citizens of Rome.

This is certainly based on the fact that Peter and Paul were martyred in Rome, however the inscription may also imply that Damasus believed both apostles had also once been buried at this site. It is known that the feast of Peter and Paul (June 29) was celebrated here, as well as at the original burial sites of the apostles. The present church of San Sebastiano is a seventeenth-century replacement of the original basilica.

In the catacombs of San Sebastiano, look for paintings of the Good Shepherd and fourth-century representations of the biblical stories of Jonah and Noah. You may also see the fish, the chi-rho with a dove (on a child's tomb), and a sarcophagus with a sculpture of Jesus raising Lazarus. The tour of the catacombs ends when you emerge into the church of San Sebastiano. In a reliquary cabinet is kept the original stone from the *Quo Vadis?* chapel, which is supposed to preserve the footprints of Jesus. Also in the church is a bust of Jesus, which may be the last work of the master Bernini.

The Catacombs of San Callisto

The Catacombs of San Callisto are named after St. Callistus, who was bishop of Rome from 217–222 CE. Before he was bishop he was a deacon, and his predecessor Bishop Zephyrinus put him in charge of managing the catacombs. After Callistus became bishop, he expanded the catacombs, and several of the third-century bishops of Rome who were martyred during the persecution of the emperors Decius and Valerian were originally buried here.

In the catacombs of San Callisto, there are some important chapels, including the Chapel of the Sacraments, which included Eucharistic paintings, and the so-called Chapel of the Popes, where nine of the third-century bishops were buried, including Zephyrinus, Callistus' successor, and Fabian, one of the first martyrs of the Decian persecution in 250. Sixtus II was martyred in these very tunnels in 258. Note Cornelius' inscription with the abbreviation EP. Also note that the inscription on the tomb of bishop Marcellinus (died 304 CE), includes the abbreviation PP, for "pope." This is probably the earliest known use of the term pope for the bishop of Rome, though the title was also used by other important bishops until the fifth century. Note the sixth-century frescoes of Cornelius and Sixtus.

There is also a late second-century painting of the Good Shepherd, along with other paintings of the fish and bread basket, Jesus' baptism, Jesus healing the paralytic and raising Lazarus. The so-called Cubiculum of the Annunciation is elaborately painted, and a child-sized sarcophagus is decorated with a sculpture of the wedding in Cana. Finally, this catacomb includes the Crypt of St. Cecilia, with paintings from the fifth through the seventh centuries. Even more remarkable is the statue of St. Cecilia, showing her as her body was found, complete with the marks of the executioner's sword on her neck. The statue in the catacombs is a copy of the original, which is in the church of Santa Cecilia (see the church of Santa Cecilia below).

The Catacombs of Domitilla
(and original Title Church of Santi Nereo e Achilleo)

According to tradition, these catacombs are named after Flavia Domitilla, who was the wife (or niece) of a Roman senator named Flavius Clemens (see the church of San Clemente below). Clemens was the first cousin of the emperor Domitian (reigned 81–96), and Domitilla was Domitian's niece. The couple's children were in line to succeed Domitian for the throne of the Flavian dynasty, until Domitian had Clemens beheaded in the year 95 on a charge of "atheism," a common epithet for Christians at that time (since they believed in only one God). Domitilla was exiled to one of the islands off the coast of Naples (just as the apostle John was exiled to the island of Patmos off the coast of what is now Turkey), where she was eventually martyred herself. Some versions of the story make Domitilla the niece of Flavius Clemens, possibly to present her as a consecrated virgin to encourage monastic vows. Perhaps there were two women named Domitilla, one was Clemens' wife and the other his niece. In any event, according to tradition, Flavia Domitilla left some of her land in the care of the Christian community, who used it to create this series of catacombs. It is difficult to know to what extent this could be true, since part of the motivation for the execution of senator Clemens might very well have been so that Domitian could confiscate his property. However, even if this happened, the property could have reverted to the family after Domitian's assassination.

The most remarkable feature of these catacombs is the remains of the original title church of Saints Nereo and Achilleo. Built mostly underground to be directly over the martyrs' tombs, the church is still used for occasional services. The church was built in the late fourth century, though the present roof is not original (the church suffered earthquake damage in the tenth century). The catacombs were probably originally named after these saints. According to tradition, Nereo and Achilleo were Roman soldiers, possibly of the praetorian guard, whose job it was to torture and execute Christians during the Great Persecution (early fourth century). However, they were moved by the fact that their victims would rather die than give up their faith, so they quit their jobs, professed their conversion to the faith, and were subsequently martyred. The title church, along with the remains of Domitilla, was actually moved to its present location near the Baths of Caracalla by Pope Leo III at the end of the eighth century. The remains of Saints Nereo and Achilleo were moved there in the sixteenth century. Unfortunately the current church of Santi Nereo e Achilleo near the baths is not open to the public, but its original site within the catacombs is still accessible.

In addition to the underground title church, visitors to Domitilla may see paintings of the Good Shepherd, a nativity scene with four magi, and a picture of Christ depicted as the mythical Orpheus. However, the tours of the catacombs do change a bit sometimes, so one cannot be guaranteed to see everything.

The Vatican Necropolis

Saint Peter's basilica is built over a necropolis (see Circus of Nero above and church of San Pietro below). This is the graveyard that was adjacent to the north side of the Circus of Nero on the Vatican Hill. After the apostle Peter was crucified in Nero's Circus, he was buried in this necropolis, and the site was remembered and visited by pilgrims from the beginning. Eventually, in the second century, a monument was built at the site, the so-called, "Trophy of Gaius." In this case, the word "trophy" means a memorial marker, like a small altar with a mantelpiece. However, according to tradition, in the middle of the third century the body of Peter was moved temporarily (along with the body of Paul) to the catacombs of San Sebastiano. If this is true, the remains were eventually returned to the original burial sites of the apostles, sometime before the turn of the fourth century. In the fourth century, one of the first churches built by the new emperor Constantine was a basilica built over the trophy, and this was the first church of Saint Peter, on the very site where the current basilica is today. In the year 595, Pope Gregory the Great (bishop 590–604) embellished the altar, as did Pope Callistus II (bishop 1119–1124), and of course it was embellished even more when the new Saint Peter's was built, but the main altar is still directly over the tomb of St. Peter.

In the early twentieth century, the area under the altar of St. Peter's basilica was excavated. The archaeologists found the remains of a first-century man, but without any remnant of the feet bones. Assuming Peter was crucified upside down, the most expedient way for the Romans to take his body down from the inverted cross would have been to cut off his feet.

The Vatican Necropolis can only be visited by making an appointment ahead of time. Only small groups are taken in with a tour guide. The main reason for going is, of course, to see the bones of the apostle Peter, which are now kept in a transparent box in their original spot. Don't expect to see a skeleton, though, since only small pieces remain of the saint's relics. In addition to this very moving experience, it is also spiritually rewarding to find yourself under and behind the high altar of St. Peter's basilica. In the mausoleums of the Vatican Necropolis, you will also see urns for cremation (which shows that this necropolis was originally in use for pagan burials), as well as some Christian symbols, like the chi rho, the Good Shepherd, Jonah, grapes, and a fisherman. Your guide will also show you a spectacular mosaic from the middle of the third century, which depicts Christ as the mythical Helios, riding across the sky in a chariot. This is the earliest Christian mosaic in existence.

The Capuchin Cemetery

Although this "attraction" is late by our standards (eighteenth century), it is worth a visit, if only for the sake of curiosity. It is found at the church of Santa Maria di Concezione, just off of Piazza Barberini, on Via Vittorio Veneto, at the corner of Via di Cappuccini. Go up the stairs to the landing on the right hand side and enter by the side door.

This is a cemetery of Franciscan friars of the Capuchin order. The monks have been here long enough that eventually they started running out of room for burying their deceased brothers. True to the medieval Franciscan spirit, they decided to make room for new burials by digging up the bones of those long dead, and using those bones to decorate a series of chapels, which are now open to the public. The dirt that you will see on the floors, and in which some of the monks are buried, is said to be from the Holy Land. The decorations you will see, including the chandeliers, are all made from human bones.

You will pass by six chapels. The Crypt of the Resurrection, with its main focus a picture of Jesus calling Lazarus out of his tomb. From the very beginning the visitor is reminded of resurrection to set the stage for what is to come. The second chapel is the so-called Mass Chapel; then the Crypt of the Skulls, with a circle of skulls and a winged hourglass, depicting the expression, *tempus fugit* (time flies). In the Crypt of the Pelvises, look for the symbols of Christ's passion: the cross with a spear and a sponge on a stick. Next is the Crypt of the Leg Bones and Thigh Bones, with the Franciscan coat of arms—literally. The two arms represent Christ (bare) and St. Francis of Assisi (with the sleeve). Finally, in the Crypt of the Three Skeletons, you will see more winged hourglasses, and a grim reaper (look up). Note the clock over the door, with only an hour hand and numbers only going up to six—the point being that time is meaningless in eternity.

One might think that the cemetery is macabre, or even sacrilegious. However, St. Francis of Assisi used to sign his letters with a drawing of a skull, to remind people of their mortality. This is the point of the Capuchin Cemetery. Actually, there are two points, two messages that the brothers hope visitors will receive. The first is that life triumphs over death. They have used death (bones) to make the point that eternity is more important than earthly time, and eternal life will triumph over death. *Oh death, where is your victory? Oh death, where is your sting* (1 Cor 15:55). The second message is given at the end of the series of chapels. St. Francis wanted to remind people of their mortality so that they would be motivated to be reconciled to God while they live, since "time flies." Thus, in the last chapel is a sign by which the bones of the monks speak to you. They warn: *What you are, we once were—what we are, you will be.*

Chapter 4

The Churches of Rome

LOOKING UP TO HEAVEN: THE APSE MOSAICS

BEFORE WE PROCEED TO the churches themselves, it will be helpful to be able to appreciate one of the most beautiful aspects of the important churches: the apse mosaics. You will be in historic churches where Christians have worshiped for centuries, and in some cases more than a thousand years. We know that the main focal point of these churches is the altar, which is often also the tomb of a martyr or other saint. The canopy, or *baldacchino*, covers the place that is the Christian "holy of holies" within the church because it is holy ground (as a tomb) and it is the place where the Eucharist is celebrated. However, when worshipers lift their eyes above the altar, they see the curved apse of the basilica, decorated with a mosaic that is meant to give them a glimpse into heaven, much like the apostle John's visions of heaven in Revelation chapters 4 and 5. In fact, much of the imagery used in the apse mosaics comes from the Book of Revelation.

Jesus Christ is usually central, of course. Even in those cases where a church is dedicated to Mary and she occupies a central space, Christ is bound to be represented in a more important role, such as crowning her (Rev 12:1). If the Trinity is represented, God the Father is often depicted as a hand coming down toward Jesus, holding a laurel wreath crown, the symbol of victory. This brings to mind Christ's victory over death in his resurrection, and also that he is the prototype of all martyrs. The Holy Spirit will virtually always be represented by a dove.

Flanking Christ are usually the two most prominent apostles, Paul and Peter, with Paul normally on the left (Jesus' right) and Peter on the right (Jesus' left). Paul is usually shown bald (or balding), with a dark pointed beard, while Peter has white hair and a curly beard. Eventually, Paul and Peter would come to be distinguished by their respective symbols: Paul with a sword (the method of his execution and a metaphor for his role in writing the Scriptures, the "double-bladed sword" of Eph 6:17, Heb 4:12, and Rev 1:16), and Peter with the keys (a metaphor for the authority to forgive sins, from Matt 16:18–19). Below Paul and Peter, in the corners, look for symbolic representations of the two cities Bethlehem (usually on the left) and Jerusalem (usually on the right). Normally, we should expect Bethlehem to be on the same side as Paul because Paul was the apostle to the Gentiles, and Bethlehem was where Gentiles (the Magi) first adored the Savior. However, this is not always consistent. Thus Bethlehem and Jerusalem come to represent Gentile Christians and Jewish Christians, respectively. Often there are sheep depicted as coming from the two cities toward Christ, the Lamb of God, in the center. The sheep, if there are twelve of them, may represent the twelve apostles, or they may represent Christians generally, who are all disciples of Christ. Ultimately, the sheep are moving toward the heavenly Jerusalem, eternal life.

Behind Christ you will see images from the Book of Revelation, such as the four winged creatures that have come to represent the four gospels. Jesus may be depicted as "coming on the clouds" (Rev 1:7) which are colored red to suggest the dawn, a reminder of his resurrection and of the promise of resurrection for all who follow him. In some early mosaics, Jesus is seated, depicted as an early bishop preaching from his chair. The apostles may be gathered around him, like the priests of the early cathedral, seated lower and closer to the congregation. When Jesus is depicted standing, however, he may be above a small hill, suggestive of Calvary, but with four rivers flowing from it. These are the four rivers of the book of Genesis, combined together with the image of the river of life from the Book of Revelation (22:1–3). The point is that the New Jerusalem (i.e., heaven), is meant to be a return to the paradise of Eden. Palm trees often frame the scene, which both add to the sense that we are looking into paradise and also symbolize the victory of resurrection over death, and of eternal life.

Rome

When the mosaic includes a cross, look for the cross to be ornately decorated or entangled in vines and leaves, as if the cross itself is a tree. This is exactly the intention portrayed in the image. The cross is the new tree of life, recapitulating a theme from the first chapters of the book of Genesis. In fact, in early Christian theology, the "tree of the knowledge of good and evil" foreshadowed the cross, in the sense that this first tree brought sin into the world, and the cross (the "tree" on which Jesus hung) was the remedy for sin. Where Adam was selfish and made himself his own highest authority, Jesus Christ was selfless and submitted himself, even to death for our sake. After the emperor Constantine legalized Christianity in the fourth century, he also discontinued the use of crucifixion as a method of execution. This facilitated a shift in the meaning of the cross, from an image of death to an image of life. It was only after this time that the cross became a symbol widely used by the church.

To the sides of Paul and Peter, we often find various other martyrs, saints, and holy people. The martyrs after whom the churches are named may be included, as well as other popular saints. Notice that the martyrs are often offering their own laurel-wreath crowns to Christ. Sometimes the apostles are presenting the martyrs to Christ. Finally, the bishop of Rome who commissioned or presided over the building of the church may be included, usually holding a model of the church itself and presenting that to Christ. Many of the people depicted in the mosaics may have halos. The halo (also called a *nimbus*) was first used only for Christ himself, signifying his divine nature. Later it was extended to Mary and the other saints to signify, not divinity but holiness. When the use of the halo was extended to pictures of others, Jesus' halo became fancier, often including a stylized cross or the Alpha and Omega. In a few places, you will see the full body halo, or *mandorla*. The square halo indicates that the person in question was still alive when the image was created, so it's a kind of provisional halo—the person is considered holy, but they have not yet entered into eternal life. Usually the square halo is found on the bishop who is presenting the church to Christ.

Finally, notice that many of the apses have a secondary set of mosaics on an arch that is either on the front of the apse or set into the building over the altar. This is meant to be a kind of Christian "triumphal arch," in the sense that it highlights the ultimate triumph of life over death, as well as the triumph of the church over the empire. Either below or above the scene, you will often see the *Agnus Dei*, the Lamb of God, sometimes with a cross or an empty throne (waiting for the return of Christ as judge).

This may be with the lambs at the bottom of the mosaic or it may be on the arch. Finally, look for other symbols from the Book of Revelation, such as the seven lampstands, or the scroll with seven seals.

SAN CLEMENTE (TITLE CHURCH)

Location

We begin with San Clemente, in part because it is one of the most spectacular sites in all of Rome and also because it contains remains of one of the earliest Christian basilicas. Visitors can enter the *scavi*, or excavations, under the church and stand in the space where Christians worshiped in the earliest centuries of the church's existence. Regardless of the amount of time one has to spend in Rome, this church is not to be missed. The church of San Clemente (or St. Clement's) is located on the Via di San Giovanni in Laterano, about a third of the way from the Colosseum toward the cathedral of San Giovanni in Laterano. It's at the corner of Via dei Querceti, at Piazza San Clemente. Notice that the original entrance on the small piazza is below street level (at the level of the street in the Middle Ages), however most people enter through the side door along the Via di San Giovanni in Laterano.

The Façade of San Clemente, as Seen from the Courtyard

The Story

The apostle Paul mentions a Clement in his letter to the Philippians (4:3). Some believe this was the senator Flavius Clemens, mentioned above (see Catacombs of Domitilla). Others, including some early Christian authors, have maintained that the Clement mentioned by Paul is a disciple of Peter who became the fourth bishop of Rome. In that role, he wrote a letter of advice (called *First Clement*) to the Christian community in the Greek city of Corinth (the same city to which Paul had written four decades earlier). The letter was probably written in the early 90s of the first century, just before the outbreak of persecution under the emperor Domitian. Some scholars date it later, since it does seem to refer to ongoing persecution in Rome, however the favorable way in which Clement talks about the emperors (their reigns are said to be ordained by God) makes it more likely that the persecution has not yet escalated.

The similarity of the name of Clement of Rome (who would be bishop from 88–97 CE) with the senator Clemens has given rise to speculation that perhaps the two were related. It has been said that Bishop Clement was once a slave in the (Christian) household of the senator, and when Clemens was executed, his will provided for the manumission of his slaves. A freed slave might take the name of his former master, so the story is plausible. However, since the senator was not executed (presumably resulting in the freedom of Clement) until 95 CE (seven years after Clement became the bishop), if the story is true that would mean that Clement was still a slave during the first part of his time as bishop. This is certainly possible, and it would mean that the church of Rome had taken Paul's words in Galatians 3:28 to heart.

According to an early legend (that goes back at least to the fourth century), Clement himself was exiled in 97 and sentenced to hard labor in the mines. There he ministered to the other prisoners, converting both prisoners and guards to Christianity. This caught the attention of the authorities and he was eventually martyred, by being tied to an anchor and thrown into the Black Sea. There is no concrete evidence from the early church that Clement was martyred, however he does seem to have been exiled from Rome, which explains why the date of his death (around 99 or 100) is later than the date that his time as bishop ended. It is possible that some confusion with the senator Clemens resulted in a story of Clement's martyrdom, however it is equally possible that he was in fact exiled to the mines and died there, either from the hard labor or from execution. In any case, the church considers him a martyr. The legend continues that in the ninth century, St. Cyril was inspired to look for the body of Clement in the Black Sea. According to the story, he found both Clement's body and the anchor on an island in the year 861, and in 867 he brought Clement's remains to Rome and presented them to Pope Nicholas I. Regardless of the truth of this legend, it appears that St. Cyril did visit Rome, and died in Rome, and he is now buried in San Clemente, along with the remains of Clement, as well as the remains of St. Ignatius of Antioch, the second-century bishop of Antioch in Syria, who was brought to Rome to be martyred in the year 110.

The Church

Since this is a title church, it is assumed that Christian worship on this site goes back to the earliest days of the church. There may have been a house church meeting on this site, and it may have been owned by the senator Clemens, who could have willed it for use by the church after his death, however we still have the problem that normally the emperor (Domitian) would confiscate all the property of a senator who was executed. There may also have been an early church meeting on this site, though not in a house but in a borrowed space, such as a warehouse. Perhaps Bishop Clement was once the pastor of this congregation. As we will see, there is a first-century warehouse beneath the church.

The first church building on this site was dedicated to the memory of St. Clement in 385 CE by Pope Siricius (bishop 384–399). This church still exists just beneath the present-day church, and you will be able to go down into it. In the sixth century, Pope John II (the first pope to change his name, since his given name was pagan: Mercurius) donated the marble *schola*, the central walled area where the "choir" of lower orders of clergy would sit. The marble chair and pulpit were donated by Pope John III in the late sixth century.

However, a series of earthquakes in the ninth century had made the original church unstable, and it was heavily damaged by the German invasion of 1084, so after some attempts at stabilizing it with brick supports, the present church was built over it in the twelfth century, by demolishing the upper level of the fourth-century church and filling it in with the rubble. The sixth-century marble furnishings of the original church were brought up to the present church in the year 1108. However, the new church was smaller than the original, which meant that the *schola* had to be cut down to a smaller size. The new church was dedicated in 1128.

In the seventeenth century, San Clemente was given as a place of refuge for Irish Dominicans who fled Protestant Britain. It was the Dominicans who would excavate the lower church in the nineteenth century and reopen it for pilgrims.

The Apse Mosaic of San Clemente

What to Look For

In the present (12th century) church, notice the apse mosaic. Although this mosaic was made in the 12th century, it is probably a copy of the original one that was done in the early 5th century. However, it is very likely the case that the original mosaic did not have the *corpus*, or the body of Jesus on the cross, and that this was a medieval addition to the earlier image of the cross. Note that the cross itself is presented as the tree of life, with the four rivers emerging from its base. The "tree" is home to "the birds of the air" (Matthew 13:31–32), including two peacocks. The inscription proclaims that the church is like a vine, reminiscent of John 15.

Paul and Peter are on the arch, along with their respective cities, rather than in the apse. St. Clement sits next to Peter. In the peak of the arch, look up to see the *chi-rho* with the letters Alpha and Omega.

Look for the seams in the walls of the *schola*, evidence that it had to be made smaller when it was brought up from the church below. There are points where the marble was cut right through the symbolic decorations. Look for eucharistic and other Christian symbols on the *schola*. Touch the marble here, and know that Christians have touched this same marble for almost 1,500 years.

The lower levels are accessed through a door in the gift shop. There is a modest entrance fee, which goes toward the upkeep of the site. As you go down, there are three distinct levels below the present church.

The Fourth Century Level

As you descend the stairs, you are now in the fourth century. You will find yourself in what was the portico (narthex) of the original church. The brickwork around the columns and along the walls was put there to support the fourth-century church after the earthquakes and invasions of the Middle Ages, as well as for additional support when the upper church was built. Moving into the main space of the basilica, be conscious of the fact that you are walking where the early Christians walked. These walls echoed their songs and their prayers. Some early Roman synods were held here, and the marble chair that is now in the church above was used by the bishop of Rome. Note that the ceiling would have been much taller, but it was cut down in order to build the twelfth-century church above. Remember that the interior space of the fourth-century basilica was originally larger than that of the present church. The supports for the upper church, and the fact that not all of this level has been excavated, give the impression of a smaller space. The frescoes you will see on the walls were done in the ninth through the eleventh centuries, and so were relatively new when the lower church was replaced by the present one. The altar is a later addition, as is the shrine to St. Cyril.

Rome

The Fourth-Century Church of San Clemente, Below the Present Basilica

The Late Second/Early Third-Century Level

As you descend to the level below the original fourth-century basilica, you enter the time of the early theologians, Irenaeus, Tertullian, and Hippolytus. Did they walk on these stones? According to tradition, there was a Christian house church here on this site at this time, possibly on land that once belonged to the family of the senator Clemens. You will walk through the remains of a Roman house of the late second or early third century. You will also see the walls of an ancient warehouse, also a possible place of Christian worship. Along the same street was a pagan temple called a *Mithraeum*. This was dedicated to the Persian god Mithras, and unlike most pagan temples, the Mithraea were meant to look like a cave, in which the worshipers shared a ritual meal. You will be able to look into the Mithraeum and see the slanted benches on which the people reclined (Romans ate in a reclining position), as well as the altar with a carving of a scene from the myth of Mithras, in which he slays a cosmic bull (there is a copy of this altar in the portico above, so you can see it up close). As you look through the gate into the Mithraeum, the room behind you was the anteroom, where the initiates sat. The cult of Mithras

The Churches of Rome

was open only to men, however in an ancient version of fraternity hazing, they made their initiates dress as women and wait outside while they ate.

The Mithraeum Below the Church of San Clemente

The Late First/Early Second-Century Level

On the lowest (and earliest) level of the excavations, archaeologists have discovered that the foundations of the buildings are built on the rubble left over from Nero's fire in 64 CE. Thus we can date these earliest buildings to just after that time, in the second half of the first century. As far as we can tell, these are Roman public buildings, however the date would be consistent with the time of senator Clemens and Bishop Clement of Rome. Recent scholarship has suggested that it was actually in the warehouse (built with the large tufa blocks) that a Christian congregation met

Rome

for worship. It is possible that Clement himself celebrated the Eucharist on this site.

An Ancient Alleyway Between a Warehouse (left) and Public Buildings or Homes (right), Below the Church of San Clemente

Prayer of St. Clement of Rome

Lord, all of our (my) hope is in your name, for you are the source of all creation. Open the eyes of our hearts so that we may know you—for you alone are the highest of the high, the holiest of the holy. You humble the proud, you confound the plans of the nations, you raise up the humble, and you humble those who try to raise themselves up . . . You alone are the Creator and guardian of the spirit and the God of the flesh, looking into the depths of our hearts and scrutinizing the works of our hands. You help those in danger, and save those in despair . . .

We ask you, Master, to be our helper and protector. Save those among us who are in distress, have mercy on the humiliated, raise up the fallen, show yourself to those in need, heal the sick, turn back those of your people who wander, feed the hungry, ransom our prisoners, raise up the weak, comfort the discouraged. Let all the nations know that you are the only God, that Jesus Christ is your Son and that we are your people and the sheep of your pasture . . .

For you, Lord are faithful to those who trust in you, merciful and compassionate. Forgive our sins and our injustices, our transgressions and our shortcomings. Do not take into account every sin of your servants, but cleanse us with the purification of your truth, and direct our steps to walk in holiness and justice and purity of heart, and to do what is good and pleasing in your sight . . .

Yes, Lord, let your face shine on us in peace for our good, so that we may be protected by your powerful hand and delivered from every sin by your outstretched arm. Deliver us also from those who hate us unjustly. Give harmony and peace to us and to all who live on the earth. . .

You are the only one who can do these things, and even greater good things for us, we praise you through the high priest and benefactor of our souls, Jesus Christ, through whom be the glory and the majesty to you both now and for all generations and for ever and ever. Amen.

(St. Clement of Rome, *Letter to the Corinthians*, first century)

SANTA CROCE IN GERUSALEMME (PILGRIM CHURCH)

Location

The church of the Holy Cross of Jerusalem is one of the seven historic pilgrim churches in Rome (along with San Sebastiano, San Lorenzo Fuori le Mura, Santa Maria Maggiore, San Paolo Fuori le Mura, San Giovanni in Laterano, and San Pietro/St. Peter's Basilica). Santa Croce is located on the eastern edge of the city, at the end of Via Santa Croce in Gerusalemme, where it meets the Viale Carlo Felice (the street that runs from Santa Croce to San Giovanni in Laterano).

Rome

Santa Croce in Gerusalemme

The Story

The church is said to be built on the foundations of a Roman palace given by the emperor Constantine to his mother, Helena, after he took control of Rome. In a way, this is her church, and she is known to the church as St. Helena. However, it is not dedicated to her, but rather to the relic of the True Cross that it contains. According to tradition, Helena made a pilgrimage to Jerusalem after her son had conquered the east and unified the empire. There she identified important locations of the passion of Christ, including his tomb, where she found the cross (probably meaning just the crossbeam). This True Cross was divided into pieces to be taken as relics to different parts of the empire. To this day, the pieces of the True Cross are closely monitored, and regardless whether one chooses to believe in their authenticity, the old cliché that if they were put back together there would be too much wood for one cross is certainly not true. In any case, relics of the True Cross were circulating in the west by the middle of the fourth century. The church of Santa Croce in Gerusalemme was built to house the relic of the True Cross, along with other relics of the passion. It was built to be a pilgrim shrine for those who could not go to the Holy Land, giving them a way to connect to the passion of Jesus through the relics.

The Church

The basilica of Santa Croce was built in the fourth century by the emperor Constantine after his mother Helena died (about 330 CE). Helena's tomb is in the church of Santa Maria in Aracoeli on the Capitoline Hill, however Santa Croce incorporates Helena's private chapel in its lower level. Eight of the columns are original from the fourth century (look for the seams in the false column bases, since the columns themselves continue on below the current floor to the original floor level). The church was renovated in the eighth and twelfth centuries, and the current floor is from the twelfth century, as is the bell tower. More renovations at the end of the fifteenth century revealed a startling discovery. In 1492, a brick was discovered that was

Santa Croce in Gerusalemme, Interior

inscribed with the words *TITULUS CRUCIS* (title of the cross). Behind this brick was hidden the "Titulus" itself—the plaque that was placed above Jesus on the cross, which said, "Jesus of Nazareth, King of the Jews" in three languages (John 19:19–22). The authenticity of this relic is of course debated, however it is known that it was venerated in Jerusalem at least since the fourth century, as it is mentioned in the pilgrimage diary of a Christian woman of that time named Egeria. In addition, all three languages are written right to left, which means it was inscribed by someone whose native language was Hebrew (or Aramaic), which would be unlikely if it were a western forgery. If it is authentic, it may have been brought back from Jerusalem during the crusades, and eventually hidden in the wall to preserve it during one of the invasions of Rome. It is now in the reliquary along with the fragment of the true cross. The brick with the inscription is on the wall in the entryway to the relic chapel.

The church was renovated again in the eighteenth century, this time it was decorated in a baroque style, which effectively obscured almost all traces of the early basilica. Unfortunately, they did not yet know the expression, *If it's not baroque, don't fix it.*

What to Look For

When you enter the church, look for the false column bases to find the columns that are original from the fourth century. Touch a column and think about all the Christians throughout the centuries who may have leaned on this column—saints and sinners alike (perhaps even Constantine himself). This church does not contain an ancient apse mosaic (no doubt it did at one time), though it does have an interesting fifteenth-century painting of Helena finding the cross. The altar is said to contain the remains of St. Caesarius, the sixth-century bishop of Arles who was instrumental in helping the church clarify its response to the Pelagian controversy and the theology of St. Augustine at the Council of Orange (529).

Going down the stairs to the right, one enters the chapel of Helena. This lower level would be the floor level of the fourth-century basilica, and this section was once part of Helena's home. The relic of the cross was originally housed in this chapel, but it has since been moved upstairs. The statue of Helena is a copy of an original in St. Peter's basilica, however even the original was probably a previously existing statue of a pagan goddess, modified to honor the emperor's mother. The dirt that one can see through an opening in the floor is said to be soil from Jerusalem. This chapel had a sister chapel in Jerusalem, built by Constantine there to house Jerusalem's fragment of the cross. Thus both chapels were said to be built on holy land.

On the other side of the church is a set of stairs leading up to the chapel of the relics. Along the stairs are pictures with explanations of what you will see. When you come to the top of the stairs, make sure to look on the wall to your right for the brick inscribed TITULUS CRUCIS. In the reliquaries are the fragment of the True Cross, the *titulus* (title plaque, or a part of it), along with what are said to be two thorns from the crown of thorns and a nail of the crucifixion. There are also reliquaries that hold what are said to be small pieces of the empty tomb and the pillar of scourging (see Santa Prassede for the rest of it), as well as the finger bone of the apostle Thomas (John 20:27). Presumably this would be the finger that touched the wounds of Jesus after his resurrection. Along the side is a larger piece of wood that is said to be the crossbeam of the cross of the "good thief" (Luke 23:40–43). In another room off to the right is a life sized replica of the Shroud of Turin, and a crucifix made to reflect the markings on the shroud.

Prayer of St. Ambrose

O Lord, who has mercy upon all, take away from me my sins, and mercifully kindle in me the fire of your Holy Spirit. Take away from me the heart of stone, and give me a heart of flesh, a heart to love and adore you, a heart to delight in you, to follow and to enjoy you, for Christ's sake. Amen. (St. Ambrose of Milan, fourth century)

Prayer for the Intercession of St. Helena

Holy and blessed St. Helena, with love and devotion you searched to find the True Cross of our Savior. Please pray for me, that I may have the same love and devotion to Jesus my Lord. Like you, may I accept the trials of life with patience and hope. With your intercession, may I carry the cross which the Lord has given me in this life, and one day may I share with you the crown of life eternal. St. Helena, finder of the True Cross, pray for us. Amen.

SANTA PUDENZIANA (TITLE CHURCH)

Location

Located on Via Urbana, just south of Via Depretis (one of the streets leading to Santa Maria Maggiore), one of the first things a visitor to Santa Pudenziana will notice is how far below street level the church is. In fact, this is the oldest title church still in use. Before going into the church, notice the *Agnus Dei* (Lamb of God) above the door. The inscription (based on John 1:29 and Revelation 5:6) says, *I am dead, yet alive, both Shepherd and Lamb. Here the Lamb redeems the world with his blood.*

The Story

According to tradition, this title church is on the site of a congregation that met in the home of a senator named Pudens (possibly the Pudens mentioned in 2 Timothy 4:21). The senator was converted to the faith by Peter, shortly after the apostle came to Rome, and Peter then stayed in the senator's home. Therefore, this site has a historic association with Peter's ministry in Rome, and in fact this church claims to have a part of a table on which Peter himself celebrated the Eucharist (the other half of the table is supposed to be in San Giovanni in Laterano). Archaeology has confirmed that the church was built into part of a home and shops (and possibly baths) owned by one Quintus Servilius Pudens. However, the house seems to be from the second century, not the first, though this does not prevent the second-century Pudens from being a descendant of the one who was a senator and convert of Peter.

According to the story, Senator Pudens had two daughters, Prassede (see the church of Santa Prassede below) and Pudenziana (also called Potentiana or Potenziana). These two sisters were also converted to the faith and made it their ministry to care for the bodies of the martyrs who had been executed. An inscription in the apse mosaic (referring to "the church of Pudenziana") has given rise to speculation that the name Pudenziana might be actually be a reference to Pudens himself, however even if true, that does not preclude his having a daughter with a name that is a feminine version of his own. Others have speculated that the sisters were actually the granddaughters of Pudens (perhaps as a way to harmonize the fact that the archeological evidence only dates back to the second century). There is no evidence that the sisters themselves were martyred, however they were eventually buried in the catacombs of Priscilla (which some say are named after the wife of Pudens). The home of the senator continued to be used for Christian worship after his death, and in the second century the Pudens house church became a place of sanctuary for hiding Christians during times of persecution. It was dedicated as a church by Pius I (bishop 142–155). Even though it had not yet been rebuilt as a basilica, it was probably remodeled at this time to accommodate more worshipers, and possibly to incorporate a baptismal font. This would have been at the same time that the famous Justin Martyr was teaching in Rome and writing his apologies for the faith.

Santa Pudenziana

The Church

The basilica was begun in the 380s, built on the foundations of the house and shops. The Caetani Chapel (the large chapel off to the left side of the main aisle) is what remains of the second-century worship space. The apse mosaic is probably from the fifth century, though the architectural remnant of the original fourth century apse is behind it. The church was dedicated by bishop Siricius (384–399), but it took until the eighth century to completely finish the structure. The remains of the two sisters were eventually brought into the city and Pudenziana's relics were divided between this church and Santa Prassede. Santa Pudenziana was renovated in the sixteenth century in a style that foreshadowed the baroque, and unfortunately at this time, the lower part of the mosaic was destroyed to make room for architectural decorations. More additions were made in the eighteenth and nineteenth centuries, including the present façade and the staircase leading down from the street.

Santa Pudenziana, Altar and Apse

What to Look For

Like San Clemente, when you enter Santa Pudenziana, you are in some ways entering the fourth century. There are two differences here, however. On the one hand, the fourth-century church of Santa Pudenziana is still in use. On the other hand, it has been decorated in a later style that obscures much of the ambiance of the ancient basilica. However, the apse mosaic is the oldest of its kind in Rome, and when you look at the images, you know that you are seeing the same thing that your brothers and sisters in the faith have seen for over sixteen hundred years in this space—the same spot, in fact, where Peter himself is said to have broken the bread.

In this early mosaic, Jesus is seated in the position of a teacher (as in Luke 4:20–21). In the early church, the bishops would preach from a sitting position, and only later when the churches were bigger did they begin preaching from a pulpit. The apostles are also seated but lower than Christ, which parallels the way the priests would sit around the bishop in the ancient cathedral. Jesus holds a book, which bears an inscription, which could be translated, "The Lord is the protector of the church of Pudenziana," or it could also be translated, "The Lord is the protector of the church of Pudens." This is why some have speculated that perhaps there was no woman named Pudenziana, and her very existence was created by a mistaken interpretation of this inscription. However, the tradition of the two sisters is probably too old and too strong not to be based on actual people.

Behind Jesus is the hill of Calvary and a cross. Notice how this is not the "old rugged cross," but a highly stylized jewel-encrusted symbol. There is evidence that in the fourth and fifth centuries there may actually have been such a monument at the site of Calvary in Jerusalem, put there by the emperor Constantine. This mosaic is one of the earliest depictions of the cross as a Christian symbol that we have. As you look at the cross, think about how the very concept of a cross had changed from a horrifying and humiliating method of execution to a symbol of forgiveness, victory, and eternal life.

Behind Jesus, and behind the cross, we see the skyline of Jerusalem. The buildings depicted were actual buildings in Jerusalem, built to commemorate the significant places that were identified by St. Helena. These buildings would have been known to pilgrims who had visited Jerusalem, and for those who could not, the mosaic gives a glimpse into the holy city. To the left of the cross is the round church of the Anastasis (also known as the church of the Holy Sepulchre), the site believed to be that of Christ's burial and resurrection (*anastasis* means resurrection in Greek). To the right of the cross is the octagonal church of the Ascension, which at one time had a hole in the roof over the site where Jesus is said to have ascended. In the mosaic, you can see that the building is tilted toward the viewer to show the hole.

In the sky above Jerusalem are the four winged creatures from the Book of Revelation, which by the second century had come to represent the four gospels. This is the earliest depiction of the symbols meant to represent the four evangelists. The human/angelic figure represents Matthew, the lion represents Mark, the calf represents Luke, and the eagle represents John. Unfortunately, parts of these images were ruined (and partially restored) in the renovations of the sixteenth century. The bottom of the mosaic was also cut off in the renovations. It would have originally included the typical Lamb of God on a small hill with four rivers flowing out, and probably also the twelve lambs coming out of the two cities toward the center.

Note that Paul and Peter are seated on either side of Jesus, Paul on the left (to Jesus' right) and Peter on the right. Behind them are two women with laurel-wreath crowns. They are probably meant to represent the two daughters of Pudens, Prassede and Pudenziana. However some claim that they are actually crowning Paul and Peter and that they are simply personifications of the Gentile church and Jewish church, respectively (we will see such a personification in the church of Santa Sabina). Notice that only Jesus has a halo—this is because the use of the halo in Christian art is still in its early stage, and at this time it is reserved only for Christ. On the other hand, some say that the crowns held by the sisters (or personifications of the church) also function as halos over the heads of Peter and Paul.

Before leaving the church, find the paintings of the two sisters burying the martyrs. One has the sisters near a well, which legend says was where they lovingly poured the blood of the martyrs, which was collected in a sponge. There is some confusion, however, over whether that well is supposed to be under the floor of this church, or the church of Santa Prassede.

The Churches of Rome

Santa Pudenziana Apse Mosaic

Prayer from an Ancient Christian Book of Hymns

I praise you, Lord, because I love you. Oh, Most High, do not abandon me, for you are my hope. I have freely received your grace, may I live by it. Those who persecute me will come, but do not let them see me. Let a dark cloud cover their eyes, and let darkness overcome them. Let them have no light to see, so that they cannot reach me. Let their plots come to nothing, so that whatever they plan will turn against them. For they have devised a plot, but it was not to be. They prepared themselves for malice, but they are powerless. My confidence is in the Lord, and I will not fear. Because the Lord is my salvation, I will not fear. He is a laurel-wreath crown upon my head, and I will not be shaken. Even if everything should be shaken, I will stand firm. And even if everything around me should perish, I will not die, because the Lord is with me, and I am with him. Amen.

(*Odes of Solomon*, second/third century)

SAN LORENZO FUORI LE MURA (PILGRIM CHURCH)

Location

The designation *Fuori le Mura* means "outside the walls," so any church with this in its name will be on the outskirts of the city, outside the old city walls. This also implies a church that was originally built over catacombs or other burial ground, since the Romans had a law against burial of the dead within the city walls. San Lorenzo Fuori le Mura is also known as San Lorenzo al Verano, and is located on the northeast edge of Rome, where the Viale Regina Elena meets the Via Tiburtina.

San Lorenzo Fuori le Mura

The Story

At the beginning of August of 258, the emperor Valerian had issued an imperial edict commanding that all bishops, priests, and deacons should be put to death. This command was carried out immediately in Rome. On August 6, the bishop of Rome, Sixtus II, was found in the catacombs and killed, along with four of the seven deacons of Rome. The Roman guards caught up with two more of the deacons later that same day. The last remaining deacon was Laurentius, known to us as St. Lawrence. The next day, on August 7, Lawrence was arrested. According to the story, the

Romans knew that Lawrence was the deacon in charge of distributing the church's offerings to the poor, so they demanded that he bring them the treasures of the church. He went away, only to return three days later with the poor and the sick of Rome, saying that these are the treasures of the church. He was then tortured to death (on August 10) by being burned on a gridiron. It is said that he mocked his executioners by saying, "Turn me over, I'm done on this side." Statues or paintings of St. Lawrence show him holding (or leaning on) a gridiron. Part of the actual gridiron, along with the chains that bound Lawrence before his martyrdom, are said to be in the church of San Lorenzo in Lucina, just off the Via del Corso. The site of Lawrence's martyrdom is marked by the church of San Lorenzo in Panisperna, not far from Santa Pudenziana.

The Church

St. Lawrence was buried in the catacombs of St. Cyriaca, which are under the church. The first church on the site was a relatively small *martyrium*, or martyr's shrine, built by the emperor Constantine over Lawrence's tomb in the year 330. This chapel was probably used for funerals but was more for pilgrims, since this was already a popular pilgrimage site. Special stairs were constructed for visitors to go down to Lawrence's tomb to be closer to the saint's remains. The first basilica on the site was built in the fifth century, by Pope Sixtus III (bishop 432–440). At this time, the pope had the parts of the catacombs above Lawrence's tomb removed (as was done with Santi Nereo e Achilleo in the catacombs of Domitilla), and the church was built around the tomb, intentionally made to have visual access to the tomb of St. Lawrence. This fifth-century church is still part of the present structure, incorporated into the part behind the mosaic arch, and one can still see the upper balconies (on the sides) which were probably originally designated for the women, to keep men and women separate in the assembly.

The church was expanded again in the sixth century, when Pope Pelagius II (bishop 579–590) brought the body of St. Stephen to Rome from Constantinople. Eventually, the remains of St. Justin Martyr were also brought here, so that the church is now actually dedicated to all three saints. The columns behind the mosaic arch are from the sixth-century expansion, but at this time, what is now the main aisle, or *nave*, of the church was still not yet there. The church as it was at that time was

Rome

basically what you see behind the mosaic arch. However it was damaged when it was ransacked during barbarian raids in the eighth and ninth centuries (churches outside the walls were especially vulnerable to attack and looting). The church was later repaired, and then it was completely renovated in the thirteenth century, when what is now the main part of the church was added. It is almost as if this church is made up of two churches put together, one from the fifth/sixth century, and one from the thirteenth century. In fact, it is said that one can see the seam between the two parts from the outside. Along the south side (the right as you look at the front), the seam is at the twelfth-century bell tower. Inside, the seam is at the mosaic arch.

San Lorenzo Fuori le Mura, Interior

What to Look For

Since this is, in effect, two churches connected back to back, there is no apse. However, the mosaic on the back side of the arch is from the sixth century, though restored in the sixteenth and seventeenth centuries. Since it faces into the sixth-century church, you will have to go up into the raised chancel area to see it (just make sure that doing so will not disrupt anything that might be going on in the church). Jesus is in the center, of course, but in this case, Peter is on the left (Jesus' right) and Paul is on the right. Notice that Peter is holding keys and Paul is holding scrolls, to represent his contribution to the Scriptures. The cities are also reversed, so that Jerusalem is still on the same side as Peter (representing the Jewish church) and Bethlehem is on the same side as Paul (representing the Gentile church). Next to Peter is St. Lawrence, with a book that says, "He distributed and gave to the poor," and next to him, Pope Pelagius II (no halo) presenting the sixth-century church to Christ. Next to Paul is St. Stephen holding a book that says, "Let my spirit go to God" (Acts 7:59). Next to Stephen is St. Hippolytus (who was also buried in this area), presenting his martyr's crown to Christ, however notice this is not the laurel-wreath crown we usually see, but a royal jeweled crown.

The floor is from the twelfth century and is a special kind of inlaid marble known as *Cosmati*, named after the family of artisans who perfected the craft. You will see this type of floor in other churches as well, though sometimes they are later reproductions. Often the small pieces of marble were salvaged (or scavenged) from ancient Roman buildings or monuments such as the Forum of Augustus. The altar is also from the twelfth century, and the bishop's chair and pulpit (technically, an *ambo*) are from the thirteenth century.

Go down the stairs to where you can see the tomb of the three saints below the altar. There is a marble slab hanging on the wall, which is said to be the slab on which Lawrence's body was laid after he died on the gridiron. The red stains are supposed to be his blood. At the back of the crypt is the tomb of Pope Pius IX (bishop 1846–1878). Pius IX is famous for, among other things, the dogmatic definition of the Immaculate Conception of Mary (*Ineffabilis Deus*, December 8, 1854). On your way out, notice the nineteenth-century fresco on the front side of the arch, which was created to commemorate the Immaculate Conception.

Be sure not to miss the cloister, which is entered through the sacristy on the right side of the church. If possible, take time for prayer and personal meditation in the cloister, and note the many inscriptions from the catacombs and elsewhere that are on the walls around the perimeter. There is a World War II bomb casing on display in the cloister. On July 19, 1943, a stray Allied bomb landed in the piazza in front of San Lorenzo, killing many people and destroying the façade of the church. The façade had to be completely rebuilt, but it is a faithful reconstruction of the thirteenth-century original. Later in 1943, a series of stamps was issued by the fascist government showing important buildings damaged by

Rome

Allied bombs, with the caption, *Hostium Rabies Dirui* ("The enemy's rage destroyed [this]"). As you leave the church, look at the columns along the nave, and you can see that they are chipped and damaged from the bomb blast, but only on the side facing the front door. An inscription in the floor remembers the date of the bombing and the reconstruction of the front of the church.

WWII Bomb Casing in the Cloister of San Lorenzo Fuori le Mura

Don't forget to look at the medieval frescoes in the portico. Finally, notice the column in the piazza in front of the church. At the top is a statue of St. Lawrence, holding his gridiron.

Prayer Attributed to St. Hippolytus

God and Father of our Lord Jesus Christ, Father of mercies and God of all consolation, you who live in the highest, but regard the lowest, you who know all things before they exist . . . Now, Lord, continue to preserve the spirit of your grace in us (me), so that being filled, we (I) may serve you in simplicity of heart, praising you, through your Son Jesus Christ, through whom all glory and power are yours, Father and Son with the Holy Spirit, in your holy church, now and throughout the ages for all eternity. Amen.

(Apostolic Tradition, third/fourth century)

Prayer for the Intercession of St. Lawrence

Oh glorious St. Lawrence, deacon and martyr, who, being subjected to the most bitter torments, did not lose your faith or your conviction in confessing Jesus Christ, pray for us (me) that we (I) will have such an active and solid faith, that we (I) shall never be ashamed to be a true follower of Jesus Christ, and dedicated Christian in word and in deed. St. Laurence, pray for us (me), that the flames of divine love may burn away all traces of vice within us (me), and that we (I) may be practical and zealous in the service of the poor. Amen.

SANTA SABINA (TITLE CHURCH)

Location

Santa Sabina is on the top of the Aventine Hill, which was one of the places in Rome where the wealthy built their homes. Of course this meant that in the barbarian invasion of 410 CE, it was also the site of a lot of looting and fire damage. The church is located along the Via di Santa Sabina, which runs west (up the hill) from the Piazzale Ugo La Malfa, overlooking the Circus Maximus. Although the church is not easily accessible apart from the walk up the hill, it is well worth the effort, especially since it is one of Rome's lesser-known treasures.

Santa Sabina

Rome

The Story

According to tradition, Sabina was an aristocratic Roman woman of the second century, who was converted to Christianity by the life and witness of her slave Serapia. Serapia was put to death for spreading Christianity in the year 126, and Sabina, refusing to give up her new faith, was martyred later in that same year. Her feast day is celebrated on August 29, which is said to be the day of her martyrdom. In the fifth century, her remains were brought to the newly built basilica on the Aventine, where she rests under the altar.

Santa Sabina, Interior

The Church

Supposedly built on the site of an early house church (though there is no real evidence connecting this site with the house of Sabina), the church of Santa Sabina is nevertheless one of the earliest Christian basilicas still in use. It was begun during the time that Celestine I was bishop of Rome (422–432). The relics of St. Sabina were brought here from the catacombs in 430, but the building was not finished until the time of Sixtus III (bishop 432–440). The columns were taken from the nearby temple of

Juno Regina. Renovations were done in the ninth century, including the present chancel area. In the thirteenth century, the church was given to the Dominican order, and it was here that St. Dominic met with St. Francis of Assisi. For a time another Dominican, St. Thomas Aquinas, lived in the adjacent monastery, and it was during this time that he wrote his commentary on Aristotle's *On the Soul*. In the seventeenth century, the interior of the church was completely built over in the baroque style, but fortunately the additions were removed and it was restored to its original state in the early twentieth century. Sadly, however, the apse mosaic did not survive, and the fresco now in the apse is from the sixteenth-century renovation. The round portraits and monochrome representations of Bethlehem and Jerusalem on the arch are from the twentieth-century restoration. Santa Sabina is now where the pope holds his Ash Wednesday service every year.

Santa Sabina Mosaic Showing the Personifications of the Jewish and Gentile Church, with Inscription of Pope Celestine

What to Look For

Perhaps the most important (though least tangible) aspect of Santa Sabina is its overall ambience. This is one of the few churches in Rome that retains the "feel" of an ancient church. Being in this church, one gets a sense of what it was like in the fifth century. Notice the inlaid eucharistic symbols over the columns. Although the apse mosaic did not survive, the mosaic on the inside of the front wall is from the fifth century, the time of Celestine (bishop 422–432). The inscription calls him, "the primary bishop of all the world." Indeed, he was instrumental in guiding the ecumenical Council of Ephesus in 431, even though he was not able to attend. On either side of the inscription are two female figures, personifications of Jewish Christianity (on the left) and Gentile Christianity (on the right), the two that come together (from "Jerusalem" and "Bethlehem") to make the one church. The mosaic tomb in the middle of the floor is quite rare. It is the tomb of the Dominican abbot, Muñoz de Zamora, who died in the year 1300.

Santa Sabina is most famous for its doors. There is an original set of doors with carved wooden panels that have survived in surprisingly good condition since the early fifth century. The panels (which are now out of order after some past attempts at restoration) depict the scenes of Christ's passion. The most important one is the panel that shows the crucifixion. This is the earliest existing artistic representation of the crucifixion. It's a bit hard to see, since it's high up on the door, but you may be able to turn on a coin-operated light to illuminate the portico and give a better view. Notice that the scene has Jesus in the middle, between the two thieves. He has long hair and a beard. The focus is not on the cross, in fact, the cross itself is not really depicted; the carving simply shows Jesus in a position that both implies the crucifixion and also suggests the *orans* position of prayer. Note that Christ is shown alive (eyes open and head held up). It was not until the Middle Ages that Christ would be shown dead on the cross.

Santa Sabina Door Panel, Showing the Earliest Known Depiction of the Crucifixion

Other panels include the resurrection (two women and an angel at the tomb), and the ascension and second coming. There is also a panel which is meant to depict scenes from the life of Moses. You can see that the face of the defeated pharaoh was replaced with a different face in the nineteenth century—it was made to look like the recently defeated Napoleon.

Santa Sabina, Portal in the Portico Wall Revealing the Dominican Tree

Before leaving Santa Sabina, turn around to look at the wall of the portico (it was behind you when you were looking at the doors). There is a hole in the wall, through which you can see a tree. It is said that St. Dominic planted a tree on that spot, and according to legend, the tree that is there now miraculously replaced the original. On the other side of the church is a nice little park, with an overlook that gives a great view of Trastevere, the part of Rome that is across the Tiber. If you have time, continue just a little farther down (southwest) along the Via di Santa Sabina to the Piazza di Cavalieri di Malta. There you will see the entrance to the headquarters of the Knights of Malta. You can't go in, but if you look through the keyhole, you'll get a surprising view.

Prayer from the Fifth Century

We (I) praise you, oh God, and we (I) acknowledge you as Lord. All creation worships you, eternal Father. All the angels, all the powers of heaven, cherubim and seraphim, sing their endless praise to you: Holy, holy, holy Lord, God of power and might, heaven and earth are full of your glory. The glorious company of the apostles praise you. The noble fellowship of prophets praise you. The white-robed army of martyrs praise you. Throughout the world the holy church acclaims you, Father of unbounded majesty, your glorious true and only Son, and the Holy Spirit, our counselor and guide.

("Canticle of the Holy Trinity," fifth century)

A Prayer for Students and Teachers by St. Thomas Aquinas

Creator of everything, true Source of light and wisdom, origin of all existence, graciously shine your light on the darkness of my understanding. Take from me the double darkness in which I have been born: the darkness of sin and the darkness of ignorance. Give me the ability to learn and understand, to remember what I have learned, and grant me the grace to be able to explain correctly what I have learned, and to express myself accurately and humbly. Guide the beginning of my work, direct its progress, and bring it to a successful completion. This I ask through Jesus Christ. Amen.

SAN PIETRO IN VINCOLI (TITLE CHURCH)

Location

The church of San Pietro in Vincoli is not far from the Colosseum, however it's up the hill to the north so it's not easily accessible from that direction. The best approach is from Via Cavour, just west of the Cavour metro stop, where you will find a medieval-looking staircase leading up from the south side of Via Cavour. At the top of those stairs is Piazza San Pietro in Vincoli, and the church.

The Churches of Rome

The Story

San Pietro in Vincoli means, "Saint Peter in chains." The New Testament includes an account of Peter's arrest in Jerusalem, around the time that the apostle James was martyred (early 40s CE). Peter was arrested and thrown into a prison cell. However, due to the prayers of the faithful, Peter was released from prison by an angel (Acts 12:1–11). The chains

The Chains of Peter, San Pietro in Vincoli

are mentioned in the text as falling off Peter's wrists at the moment the angel spoke. After Peter came to Rome, he was eventually also arrested there and imprisoned. According to tradition, one of Peter's guards was converted to Christianity, and after Peter's martyrdom, this guard saved the chains that had held him. In the second century, a chapel was built (possibly on the site of an earlier house church) as a shrine for the chains that bound Peter in Rome. Legend has it that when the empress Eudocia (wife of Theodosius II) made a pilgrimage to the Holy Land in the year 438, she found the chains which had held Peter in Jerusalem (and had also been saved) and had them sent to Rome. When Pope Leo I (bishop 440–461) brought the two sets of chains together, they were miraculously joined into one, and the present church was built to commemorate this event, and house the chains of Peter. Even assuming the possibility of the miraculous, the story is a bit hard to believe. The legend of the joining of the two sets of chains probably comes from a time when there was a dispute over which set of chains this was (those from Jerusalem or Rome). Nevertheless, it is not impossible that the very chains which held Peter in Rome before his crucifixion were actually preserved.

Peter's tomb is not here, of course. It is under the altar of St. Peter's basilica in the Vatican. The relics under the altar of this church are said to be the remains of the Maccabean martyrs (2 Maccabees 7).

The Church

The church was built in the middle of the fourth century (about 340–350 CE). It was originally called the Church of the Holy Apostles, dedicated to both Peter and Paul. The basilica was later renovated by its pastor, a

San Pietro in Vincoli, Interior

priest named Philip, who was the pope's representative at the ecumenical council of Ephesus in 431. It was further renovated by Sixtus III (bishop 432–440). In the time of Leo (probably coinciding with the legend of the joining of the chains), the name was changed to Saint Peter in Chains. Further renovations took place in the eighth, fifteenth, and nineteenth centuries, covering over most of the original appearance of the basilica.

What to Look For

The main feature of this church, apart from the fact that it is a very ancient worship space, is, of course, the relic of the chains of Peter. Whether or not one believes that these chains actually held the apostle, this is a good time to pause and think about the sacrifice made by those who followed Christ and passed on the faith in the early days. In fact, there are still places in the world where living the gospel is dangerous, even life-threatening.

Michelangelo's Moses (detail), San Pietro in Vincoli

San Pietro in Vincoli is also the home of Michelangelo's statue of Moses. It was made in 1515, and was supposed to be the focal point of a much larger monument, which is why it seems big for the space. Notice the horns on Moses' head. The addition of this interesting aspect of the sculpture is based on a literal reading of Exodus 34:29–30. The Hebrew text uses an uncommon expression that is usually translated "radiant," but literally means, "horned." Most people assume that the "horns" are meant to represent the rays of light said to have shone from Moses' face when he came down from his mountaintop meeting with God. However one has to keep in mind that in the ancient world, the presence of horns did not necessarily imply evil, but rather divinity. So the image could signify that in a way some of God's divine glory had "rubbed off" on Moses. Make sure you turn on the coin-operated light so you can see the statue better.

Prayer of St. Jerome

Lord, you have given us your word for a light to shine on our path. Grant us so to meditate on that word, and to follow its teaching, that we may find in it the light that shines more and more until that perfect day, through Jesus Christ our Lord. Amen.

(Attributed to Jerome, fourth century)

Prayer for the Intercession of St. Peter

Oh glorious apostle, who received the power of binding and releasing from Christ, and who would endure imprisonment and chains for his sake, pray for us, that we might be free from all sin, so that we may live and die in the grace of God. Intercede for us that we might have a perfect faith, a firm hope, and an unfailing love for God and neighbor, that as we draw nearer to the close of life, we may daily grow in the knowledge and love of Jesus Christ. Pray for us, oh blessed apostle, that we will be guided through all the dangers of this exile, till fear and grief is no more. Oh humble martyr of Christ, you who now see him, not as on the mount of transfiguration, but in the full splendor of his glory, pray for us now and at the hour of death. When that time comes, blessed apostle, present us to Jesus, that we too may see him, and be in his eternal love. Amen.

SANTI COSMA E DAMIANO

Location

The church of Saints Cosma and Damiano backs up against the Roman forum, and is connected to the third-century-BCE temple of Jupiter Stator (Romulus). The interior of the temple is visible through a glass wall at the back of the church. However, the church is entered from outside the forum, from the Via dei Fori Imperiali, just a bit south of the intersection with Via Cavour.

The Entrance to the Church of Santi Cosma e Damiano

The Story

According to tradition, Cosma and Damiano were twin brothers from Arabia, both surgeons, who lived Christ's command to love one's neighbor by offering their medical services without charge. Some miraculous cures were attributed to the power of their prayers. Living in the East in the late third century, they are credited with having converted many people to the faith. However, they attracted the attention of the authorities and were arrested. They refused to make the required pagan sacrifices and on September 27, in the year 287, they were executed. Legends of their martyrdom include typical stories of miraculous protection (requiring several attempts at killing them). They became popular martyr-saints and there are several churches dedicated to them throughout the world.

Santi Cosma e Damiano, Interior

The Church

In the sixth century, the barbarian king Theodoric gave part of the Forum of Peace (Vespasian) to Pope Felix IV (bishop 526–530). One of the buildings of the forum was used as the foundation for the church of Santi Cosma e Damiano. This may have been the library, or as some have speculated possibly the office of the Urban Prefect. If the latter, then this church may actually be on the very site where Christians were confronted by the Roman authorities and given the choice to deny the faith or face execution.

In the eighth century, Pope Adrian I (also known as Hadrian) expanded the church and designated it a *diakonia*, a rest stop for pilgrims and a site for distributing food to the poor. In the seventeenth century, flooding required that the floor be raised. At that time, the original floor level became the crypt where the remains of the martyr twins are said to be entombed. However, the renovation that came with raising the floor resulted in the loss of the bottom part of the apse mosaic.

Santi Cosma e Damiano, Apse Mosaic

What to Look For

The mosaic in the apse is the original one from the early sixth century, which makes it one of the earliest in existence (along with the one in Santa Pudenziana). In spite of the fact that the some parts are now lost, it remains one of the most spectacular examples of Christian mosaic anywhere. Notice that Jesus is standing, and in fact seems to be floating on air. The red clouds behind him suggest the dawn of his second coming. This is one of the earliest depictions of Jesus as the long-haired, bearded (older) Jesus. This is consistent with the depiction of Jesus on the door of Santa Sabina, and is probably meant to portray him in the role of the wise teacher/philosopher. Note that he holds a scroll in his hand, which represents the Scriptures as revelation from God (remember that Jesus himself is called the Word of God in the gospel of John). The twelve lambs below Jesus represent the twelve apostles, all moving toward the Lamb of God, who stands on the hill of Calvary, which is flowing forth with the rivers of paradise.

Paul is on the left, but with Jerusalem down in the left corner; and Peter is on the right, with Bethlehem down in the right corner. The apostles are presenting the two brothers Cosma and Damiano to Christ, but since the brothers are twins, there is no way to know who is who. The brothers present their laurel-wreath crowns to Jesus. On the far left is Pope Felix IV presenting the church to Christ (the figure of Felix was restored in the seventeenth-century renovations). On the far right is St. Theodore, a Christian soldier from the time of the Great Persecution who was martyred on February 17, in the year 306. Note that Jesus is still the only one with a halo, however from the time of the mosaic of Santa Pudenziana, we have advanced from Jesus seated to standing.

Notice the phoenix in the palm tree on the left. Also note the triumphal arch, done at the turn of the eighth century, which contains images from the Book of Revelation, including seven lampstands, a scroll with seven seals in front of the Lamb of God, and the four winged creatures that represent the four gospels (only two are visible—the other two were covered over by the renovations in the seventeenth century). The centerpiece above the altar is a twelfth-century icon of the Madonna and Child.

Since this is the church of the surgeon-saints, take a moment to pray for those you know who are struggling with illness. Also pray for their doctors, and any doctors you may know, that God will continue to grant them the skill and wisdom to heal the sick.

Prayer from the Sixth Century

To God be glory, to the angels honor, to Satan confusion, to the cross reverence, to the church exaltation, to the departed quickening, to the penitent acceptance, to the sick and infirm recovery and healing, and to the four quarters of the world great peace and tranquility, and on us who are weak and sinful may the compassion and mercies of our God come, and may they overshadow us continually. Amen.

(Syriac Liturgy, sixth century)

Prayer for the Intercession of Saints Cosma and Damiano

O physicians of souls, saints Cosma and Damian, stand before the Lord of all and ask him to heal me and all those dear to me of any spiritual ills we may endure. Pray that God will drive away from us all sin and sadness of mind, all darkness and despair. Pray that we will then be made willing and loving servants of Christ, following your holy example of detachment from the things of this world and care for the needs of our neighbors. On the glorious day of the universal resurrection may we shine with you in the full health of our nature restored by the mercies of Jesus who lives and reigns forever and ever. Amen.

SANTA MARIA IN COSMEDIN

Location

This is the ancient Forum Boarium, between the Aventine, Palatine, and

Santa Maria in Cosmedin

Rome

Capitoline hills along the river. If the top of the Aventine was the residence of the wealthy, the foot of the Aventine was the residence of the poor, and parts of this area were a marshy slum. The church of Santa Maria in Cosmedin is at the intersection of the Via Teatro di Marcello (Via Petroselli, at this point) and the Via della Greca. The piazza in front of the church is the Piazza Bocca della Verità. The church faces the two Forum Boarium temples, Hercules and Portuna.

The Story

The area of the Forum Boarium would eventually become the "Little Athens" of Rome, home to a community of Greek immigrants. As far as we know, there has been a church dedicated to the Virgin Mary on this site since at least the sixth century, though some say this has been a site of Christian worship since the third century. However we also know that there was a pagan temple adjacent to the site. The original church is referred to as *Santa Maria in Schola Graeca*, or "Saint Mary of the Greek Community." The portico is from this original church, and remains one of the oldest parts of the present church. In the eighth century, Pope Adrian I (bishop 772–795) designated it a *diakonia* (like Santi Cosma e Damiano) to help feed the hungry poor of the area.

Santa Maria in Cosmedin, Interior

The Church

Pope Adrian enlarged the church, creating the basilica you see today. In doing so, he cut down the parts of the adjacent pagan temple that were still above ground, however remains of the temple can still be seen below the church in the crypt. The remains of martyrs brought into the city from the catacombs were placed in the crypt. Adrian then presented the church to the Greek community, which was swelling with numbers of Greek-speaking immigrants who had fled the persecution of the iconoclasts in the East. There is some disagreement over the meaning of the word *Cosmedin*, however it seems to have something to do with the fact that it was considered a beautiful church at the time. The church was then expanded again in the ninth century, but was later damaged in the German invasion of 1084. It was renovated in the twelfth century, including the addition of the medieval bell tower. Baroque decorations and a new

Santa Maria in Cosmedin, Baldacchino and Apse

façade were added in the eighteenth century, but thankfully these were removed in the twentieth century (like Santa Sabina). Therefore, the interior of the church that you see today is very much as it would have looked in the eighth and ninth centuries, with some additions from the twelfth and thirteenth centuries.

What to Look For

As you enter Santa Maria in Cosmedin, you will see that (like Santa Sabina) this is one of the few churches left anywhere that gives a person the feeling of being in an ancient church. Imagine the people standing in the side aisles (men on the right, women on the left). Curtains hang between the columns, separating the side aisles from the nave. The priest(s) and deacon(s) would be in the chancel, with another curtain across the front. Consecrated widows and monastics, along with others who were considered lower orders of church leaders, would be in the *schola cantorum* (choir gallery) in the center. More curtains hang from the crossbeams of the *schola*, and in fact the whole church would have been decorated with curtains, tapestries, linen tablecloths, and cushions. The catechumen (those not yet baptized) along with those who are in the process of doing penance, are in the back of the church, possibly separated by another curtain (perhaps some curtains were opened or closed at particular parts of the liturgy). There are no chairs or pews however. The people stand for worship, with the exception of the penitents who are expected to kneel. Another set of curtains hangs from the *baldacchino* (or *ciborium*), the canopy over the altar. The curtains are meant to convey the mystery of the sacrament. Perhaps there were multiple sets of curtains, with finer silk curtains reserved for important holy days.

Unfortunately, the original apse mosaic did not survive, however the painting in the apse is meant to represent what the apse would have looked like with the earlier mosaic. The *schola* is from the twelfth century. The *baldacchino* was added in the late thirteenth century. In the chapel of the Madonna (also called the Chapel of the Choir), there is a thirteenth-century painting of *The Mother of God Ever Virgin*. This painting was the centerpiece over the main altar until the seventeenth century. In another chapel is a relic—the skull of St. Valentine (the rest of him is in a Carmelite church in Dublin and was a gift from Rome to the Catholics of Ireland).

The Skull of St. Valentine, Santa Maria in Cosmedin

The crypt is worth a visit, though there may be a small charge for entry. This (along with the portico) is probably what's left of the original sixth-century church. When Pope Adrian built the present basilica in the eighth century, the adjacent pagan temple was destroyed, and the sixth-century church became the crypt. The columns and side wall of the crypt are what remains from the pagan temple (note that the columns continue on below the floor, demonstrating that the floor level of the temple was below the floor level of the sixth-century church).

Before leaving the church, stop in the gift shop. On the wall is a fragment of a mosaic from the eigth century. It is part of the scene of the adoration of the Magi, and it was originally in the old St. Peter's basilica.

Finally, in the portico is the famous *La Bocca della Veritá*, "the Mouth of Truth." It is a round sculpture of a Roman god, five feet in diameter, weighing over a ton. It's propped up on a discarded column capital in the courtyard, and it has become quite a tourist attraction. It was once thought to be a sewer cover (probably because it's round with holes in it), and so it was assumed to be a depiction of a water god, such as Neptune. However, recently there is more debate over just what it is, some saying it is actually a fertility god. Notches for brackets on the backside suggest it was always meant to be hung on a wall. It may be from the ancient temple that was once adjacent to the sixth-century church on this site. If so, it could be as much as 2,500 years old. The sculpture was put here in the portico in the seventeenth century. A legend of unknown origin (but made famous by the 1953 film *Roman Holiday*) says that anyone may place a hand in the mouth of this anonymous god—but the hand of a liar will be bitten. That's why it's the "Mouth of Truth." Many tourists line up to have their picture taken with their hand in the mouth; sadly many of them will never enter the church.

Prayer from the Sixth Century

Awaken us, oh Lord, from the sleep of apathy and from tossing to and fro in our thoughts, so that we may no longer live as in a troubled dream but as people awake and resolved to finish the work you have given them to do. By your humble birth, root out of our hearts all pride and haughtiness, that humble ways may content us, so that we may serve the humble. By the life of compassion for those who labor and are heavy laden, teach us to be concerned one for another and to bear one another's burdens. By your hallowed and most bitter anguish on the cross, make us to fear you, and love you, and follow you, oh Christ. Amen.

   (St. Brigid of Ireland, sixth century)

Fourth Century Prayer for the Interecession of the Virgin Mary

O sovereign Virgin, noble and blessed lady, you dwell in heaven, in the abode of the elect. You have shaken off the burden of human existence to be clothed in the apparel of immortality. We know that like God, you are ever young. In the heights of heaven, accept my prayers with kindness. Among all mortal beings, you alone possess the privilege of being Mother of the Word, in a way beyond all understanding. For this reason, I place my confidence in you. Protect me always from every evil, from visible enemies and even more, from invisible foes. May I cross the last threshold of my life as I have begun it, with you ever as my guardian. Be, at all times, my all-powerful advocate with your Son, in the company of those holy ones so pleasing to him. Do not allow me to be delivered up to torture for having been the puppet of the evil one, the corrupter of souls. Protect me, preserve me from flames of fire and from darkness. Let the faith and grace that are yours be efficacious for my justification, for it is well known that God's grace comes to us through your intercession. Amen.

   (St. Gregory of Nazianzus, fourth century)

Prayer for the Intercession of Saint Valentine

Dear saint and glorious martyr, Valentine. Pray for us, that we will learn to follow your example, and love unselfishly, finding great joy in giving. Pray that all true lovers will bring out the best in each other. Love is patient and kind, it doesn't envy or boast and it's never proud. Love is not rude or selfish. It doesn't get angry or keep track of wrongs. Love doesn't delight in bad things, but it rejoices in the truth. Love always protects, trusts, hopes, and preserveres. Love never fails.

(Adapted from the apostle Paul's *First Letter to the Corinthians*, first century)

SANTA PRASSEDE (TITLE CHURCH)

Location

Santa Prassede, also called Praxedes in some sources, is not far from its sister church of Santa Pudenziana, in the area around Santa Maria Maggiore. However, the façade of Santa Prassede is obscured by the surrounding buildings, so the entrance is now along the side, on a small street called Via Santa Prassede that runs parallel to the Via Merulana, between Via dell' Olmata and Via San Martino ai Monti. Because it can be somewhat hard to find, the best way to approach is from the southern corner of Santa Maria Maggiore. Facing south, the street that is just to the right of Via Merulana and heads southeast is Via Santa Prassede.

The Story

Prassede was the other daughter of the Roman senator Pudens. Although Santa Prassede is considered a title church, the house of Pudens is not here, it is beneath Santa Pudenziana. The church of Santa Prassede may also be situated over an early house church, though some sources confuse this site with the house of Pudens. In any case, the senator and his daughters were said to be converts of the apostle Peter, who stayed with them while he was in Rome (note the painting of Peter at the house of Pudens—Peter is shown holding a red book with keys draped over it). According to tradition, the two sisters collected and cared for the bodies of the martyrs who were executed. It is said that Prassede in particular made a habit of lovingly taking up the martyrs' blood in a sponge

The Entrance to Santa Prassede

and then pouring it into a well. Therefore, Prassede is often depicted in paintings holding a sponge or sitting near a well. Different versions of the story disagree as to whether the well was at the house of Pudens under Santa Pudenziana, or on this site, however this basilica appears to have been built around an ancient well, and today the red marble circle in the floor marks the spot where the well used to be. The bodies of the martyrs that were retrieved by the two sisters were said to be placed in the catacombs of Santa Priscilla, though this cannot be verified, since it is not clear that these catacombs were in use yet in the first century. In reality, the connection between the two sisters and the catacombs of Priscilla may explain why some versions of the story make them the granddaughters of Pudens rather than his daughters. The senator and his daughters were eventually also laid to rest in the catacombs of Priscilla.

The Churches of Rome

Santa Prassede, Interior

The Church

The first church on this site was built in the fourth or fifth century, possibly on the site of an earlier place of Christian worship. However, nothing of this church remains, with the possible exception of parts of the Chapel of Zeno. The present basilica was built in the ninth century by Pope Pascal I (bishop 817–824), during a time known as the Carolingian Renaissance. At this time, Charles the Great (Charlemagne) had created the empire of Europe (the so-called Holy Roman Empire), and instituted a standardization of Christian liturgy in the west. Pope Pascal's role was to try to bring back the glory of Constantinian Rome, and to that end, churches like Santa Prassede and Santa Cecilia were made to emulate the fourth and fifth-century churches. Therefore, it is likely that the present church of Santa Prassede is not much different from the fourth or fifth-century version, though perhaps more ornate. In fact this basilica was meant to be a smaller copy of the original St. Peter's basilica.

Pascal made an effort to bring the remains of the martyrs into the city from the catacombs. This was a time when invasions could make visiting the catacombs dangerous, and certainly the relics of the martyrs

129

were in danger of theft or desecration. The remains of the two sisters were brought to Santa Prassede, and now share a sarcophagus in the crypt below the altar (actually, only part of the remains of Pudenziana are here, the rest of her is under the altar of the church dedicated to her).

The Apse and Triumphal Arches of Santa Prassede

What to Look For

The apse mosaic is the original one from the ninth century. It was created to follow the style of the earlier ones, such as in Santi Cosma e Damiano. Jesus Christ stands among the clouds, with the Jordan River at his feet. As in the earlier mosaic, Paul is on the left, Peter on the right, with Bethlehem and Jerusalem in the corners. Paul presents Prassede to Christ, while Peter presents Pudenziana. To the left of Paul is Pope Pascal, presenting the church. Note the square halo, which indicates that Pascal was alive when this mosaic was made. In the palm tree over Pascal's head is a phoenix. To the right of Peter is St. Zeno, a fourth-century bishop of Verona and martyr. It is possible that the earlier fourth or fifth-century church was dedicated to him, or at least held his tomb. The main chapel off the nave to the right is named for him. Notice that Jesus' hand is showing the nail hole, marked as a red X. Above Jesus' head is the heavenly hand which represents God the Father, holding the laurel-wreath crown of Christ's victory over death.

Notice how by this time, however, everyone has a halo (even Pascal), but Jesus' halo is distinctive because it contains a cross. Unfortunately, the elaborate eighteenth-century *baldacchino* obscures part of the mosaic from view and prevents one from seeing the whole thing from the front. There should be a coin-operated light that will illuminate the mosaic.

You will notice that this church has a double triumphal arch, with mosaics that continue the themes from the Book of Revelation. On the arch attached to the apse, we see the Lamb of God enthroned, along with the seven lampstands, and the four winged creatures representing the four gospels. The sides of the arch show the white-robed martyrs of Revelation 6:11, all presenting their crowns to their Lord. The second arch (closer to you as you look from the nave) shows the heavenly city of the New Jerusalem, depicted with its walls and two gates guarded by angels. On either side, the faithful departed wait to enter, the one hundred forty-four thousand from the Jewish church on the left (Rev 7:4–8), and the countless multitudes from the Gentile church on the right (Rev 7:9–17). The small doors that are cut into the mosaics on this arch were added later, in the sixteenth century, for the display of relics on certain feast days (part of the Catholic response to the Protestant Reformation). Both arches are signed with the monogram of Pope Pascal.

Santa Prassede, Apse Mosaic

Below the apse mosaic is a painting of Prassede and her sister pouring the blood of the martyrs down the well. Prassede holds the sponge as she looks up to heaven. The columns on the sides of the chancel are from the first century, and are similar to the images of columns painted on the walls in the House of Livia.

The small crypt can be entered from the stairs in front of the altar. The remains of Prassede and Pudenziana are in one sarcophagus, and another holds the remains of several martyrs brought from the catacombs in the time of Pascal, some of them anonymous. There is a plaque on one of the pillars on the right hand side of the nave, which lists the names of many of the martyrs whose remains were transferred to the church from the catacombs. The plaque is partly reconstructed, but the upper part is original from the time of Pope Pascal. Before leaving the crypt, note the small altar. Parts of this altar are from the original fourth/fifth-century church, and the fresco above the altar, while not original, is a copy of the one from the original church. Touch the front panel of this small altar, and you're touching the first church on this site. Touch the sarcophagus of Prassede and Pudenziana, and you're touching a relic of the martyrs of the early church.

As you emerge from the crypt, look for the plaque on the pillar with the names of the martyrs. Also, notice the floor. It's not original but was done in the twentieth century, copying the *Cosmati* style. The red porphyry circle marks the supposed site of the well. The inscription says, "The repository of the relics of the holy martyrs, in the temple of Saint Prassede." Also in the floor is the tomb of John the Pharmacist, a fourteenth-century pilgrim (notice the bag, traveling hat, and walking stick). The inscription around the tomb is reminiscent of the sign at the end of the Capuchin Cemetery. It says, *Vos estis, ego fui; Q[uod] sum, vos eritis* ("What you are, I was; What I am, you will be").

The side chapels include the tomb of Cardinal Pantaleono Anchier, who was assassinated on this spot in 1286; the chapel of St. Charles Borromeo, including a table from which he fed the poor; as well as the chapel of St. John Gualbert, known for forgiving the man who murdered his mother. This chapel includes an interesting twentieth-century mosaic of the Holy Trinity crowning Mary.

The main chapel on the right side of the nave is the Chapel of St. Zeno, the fourth-century bishop and martyr depicted in the apse mosaic. The mosaics on the outside of the chapel seem to predate the other mosaics from the ninth century (except for the two lower corners), and it is possible that they were part of the previous church, which held the tomb of St. Zeno. Note that the doorway to this chapel is put together from older pieces, some as old as the first century. When the present church was built by Pope Pascal, this chapel was built to house the tomb of his mother, Theodora. However she was still alive when the chapel was built because she is depicted in a mosaic with a square halo.

Entering the chapel, you come into a small room decorated with mosaics on all sides. Look for the mosaic with Theodora in the square halo. The inscription calls her "Episcopa," a feminine form of the word for bishop. The three other women with Theodora are Mary and the two sisters, Prassede and Pudenziana. Above them is the Lamb of God with the rivers of Revelation 22:1. Above that is another mosaic of the two sisters with St. Agnes. On the next wall to the left, look for a mosaic of Peter and

The Holy Column, Church of Santa Prassede

Paul (this time Peter is on the left). They are gesturing to an empty throne, an image meant to bring to mind the fact that the church waits for Christ to return as judge. Moving to the next wall, we see the apostle John holding a book, with Andrew and James holding scrolls. Their hands are covered, which is an ancient indication that they are presenting gifts, as one would do in an audience with royalty. In a small apse-like niche is a mosaic that may be earlier than the rest. Some date it to the sixth century, others as late as the thirteenth century. It shows Mary with the child Jesus on her lap. To the left (Mary's right) is St. Prassede, and to the right is St. Pudenziana. Jesus holds a scroll which reads, *Ego sum lux*, "I am the light (of the world)."

The main reliquary in the chapel holds the Holy Column, also known as the Column of Flagellation. This is said to be the column to which Jesus was tied when he was whipped by Pontius Pilate's guards (John 19:1). According to tradition, it was venerated in Jerusalem until it was brought to Rome during the time of the crusades. You'll notice that it's relatively short, which shows that it was not the kind of column that held up part of a building, but was a short post used to tie up horses or donkeys. It is said that the column once had an iron ring on the top, but that was traded in the thirteenth century for three thorns from Jesus' crown of thorns (two are now on display in the church of Santa Croce in Gerusalemme). You can see that a piece was chipped off of the column—this was given as a gift to the city of Padua in the sixteenth century. There is a column in Jerusalem that also claims to be the column of Jesus' scourging, which led some to speculate that the two competing columns were two halves of one original, however the column in Santa Prassede does not appear to be part of a larger one, and in fact they are made of two completely different kinds of marble. Note that in the Renaissance paintings of Jesus' flagellation, often the column is painted to look like this one.

Prayer from the Seventh Century

Grant, O Lord, that the light of your love may never be dimmed within us (me). Let it shine forth from our (my) warmed heart(s) to comfort others in times of peace and in seasons of adversity, and in bright beams of your goodness and love may we (I) come at last to the vision of your glory, through Christ our Lord. Amen.

(St. Columbanus, seventh century)

SANTA CECILIA (TITLE CHURCH)

Location

Santa Cecilia is in the area of Rome known as Trastevere (pronounced, *Tras-TAY-ve-ray*). The word means, "across the Tiber," because this is the area on the west side of the River Tiber, at a bend in the river south of the Vatican. Trastevere was at one time one of the poorer areas of Rome, and in the first century it would have been home to many of the Roman Jews, and therefore also to many of the first Roman Christians. The best way to get to Trastevere is to cross at Tiber Island, where it's very pedestrian-friendly. You can also cross at any one of a number of bridges, however be careful because a few of the bridges are difficult for pedestrians. If you do cross at Tiber Island, you will enter Trastevere from the Ponte Cestio. Santa Cecilia is straight in from there, though you will have to make a few turns to get to Via Santa Cecilia, where you can enter the courtyard and the church.

Santa Cecilia

Rome

The Story

According to tradition, Cecilia was a Christian woman, the daughter of a Roman senator, probably during the time that Urban I was bishop of Rome (222–230 CE). Her mother may have been a Christian, as it seems she was raised in the faith from a very young age. She was engaged to a pagan man named Valerianus, however she had made a personal vow of celibacy as a sign of her devotion to Christ. During the wedding, while the musicians played, she is said to have sung of her love for God alone. On the wedding night, she told her new husband that she intended to remain a virgin for Christ. Understandably disturbed by this, Valerianus demanded to see the bishop, but after meeting bishop Urban, he was converted to the faith. Valerianus then told his brother Tiburtius about Christianity, and he also converted. Cecilia, Valerianus, and Tiburtius began a ministry of helping the poor of Trastevere, feeding the hungry and caring for the bodies of those who were martyred. It appears that there was also a house church meeting in their home. Eventually, the two brothers were arrested and taken to face the urban prefect, who condemned them to execution. However, the officer who was supposed to carry out the sentence, one Maximus, was himself converted by their conviction and their bravery, and eventually all three of the men were martyred. Cecilia had them buried in the catacombs of San Callisto, which some sources say was on land originally owned by Cecilia's family. Before Cecilia herself was arrested, she made arrangements for the church to be able to continue to worship in her home. After her arrest and confession, she was condemned to death by suffocation. It is said that the first attempt to execute her was to suffocate her in her own private baths (like a steam room built into the house). After locking her in and turning up the heat, her would-be executioners waited for her to die. Instead, they only heard the sound of her singing coming from inside the bath. Finally they grew impatient, and the order was given for her to be beheaded. The executioner, apparently unnerved by Cecilia's slight frame and strong faith, swung the sword three times, but was unable to finish the task. It is said that Cecilia finally bled to death, but by some accounts it took three days. Of course the number three (in both the swings of the sword and the time it took her to die) is not a coincidence—the number is meant to connect her to her Lord, the proto-martyr, who rose on the third day, as well as to the Christian understanding of God as Trinity. But we must keep in mind that although legendary details have certainly been added to the story, that does not negate the historical existence of the martyrs in question. Cecilia was buried in the catacombs of San Callisto. Her feast day is November 22, and she is now considered the patron saint of musicians.

Santa Cecilia, Interior

The Church

The Church of Santa Cecilia is a title church, which implies that there was once an early house church on this site. In fact, archaeologists have excavated a third-century Roman house underneath the church, which could very well be the house of Cecilia. It seems that the house was dedicated as a worship space by bishop Urban, or perhaps by one of his successors after Cecilia's death. A basilica was built on the site in the fourth century, which was restored in the ninth century by Pope Pascal, the same pope who is responsible for Santa Prassede, and in fact you can see Pascal's monogram in the mosaic here, just as in Santa Prassede. The remains of all four martyrs: Cecilia, Valerianus, Tiburtius, and Maximus, as well as of Pope Urban, were all brought here from the catacombs by Pope Pascal, and are entombed under the altar. In the year 1599, the body of

Rome

Cecilia was exhumed as part of some restorations that were being done. Her body was found incorrupt, still in the position in which it was found in the catacombs before being transferred to the church. The sculptor Stefano Maderno (1576–1636) was there to witness the body as it was exhumed, and he created the sculpture of her based on what he saw. More renovations were done in the eigteenth and nineteenth centuries, to which we owe the current baroque decorations.

Santa Cecilia Apse Mosaic

What to Look For

The mosaic in the apse is from Pascal's restoration in the ninth century. Like Santa Prassede it was intentionally made to reflect the tradition of the earlier mosaics. Notice Paul and Peter, with their respective cities, and the lambs moving toward Christ, as usual. Here you can see even more clearly that the lambs are coming out of the two cities. Next to Paul on the left is St. Agatha, and then Pope Pascal presenting the church to Christ, with his square halo, which of course means he was still alive when this mosaic was made. Next to Peter on the right is the couple Valerian and Cecilia holding their martyrs' crowns. Also notice the phoenix in the palm tree over Pascal's head.

Santa Cecilia Apse Mosaic (detail, with Phoenix)

In front of the altar is Maderno's stunningly beautiful sculpture of Cecilia. This is the original (the one in the catacombs is a copy, marking the spot where her body was originally buried). Notice that Maderno saw where the sword cut her neck. Also notice that Cecilia's hands are in a position that indicated the Trinity—three fingers on her right hand and one finger on her left symbolize the God who is three in one. The inscription in the marble in front of the statue contains the words of Maderno: "See for yourself the image of the most holy virgin Cecilia, whom I myself saw lying incorrupt in her tomb. I have expressed for you this same image in this marble in the very same posture of her body."

On the right-hand side of the church, toward the back, is the Chapel of the Calidarium (hot bath), also called the Chapel of St. Cecilia, which is said to be built from the remains of part of Cecilia's bath.

On the left-hand side in the back is a small gift shop, though which you can go down into the excavation of the third-century Roman house. This may actually be more than one house, with some warehouse space as well (look for the storage vats, possibly for grain or some other commodity). The ornate crypt behind the gate is mostly from the turn of the twentieth century, however the *confessio* under the altar (behind the altar of the crypt) is the original from the ninth century. If you are able to get into the crypt, make sure to walk around behind the *confessio* to see the ninth-century mosaics of the martyrs. As you explore this third-century Roman house, consider that you are walking on the very floor that Cecilia herself, or other early Christians, walked on. Consider that this may have been a place of worship, where your ancestors in the faith prayed and received the sacraments. Touch the floor and walls and feel the connection to the cloud of witnesses who once shared many of the same loves and fears as you but who lived all those centuries ago.

Moderno's Statue of Saint Cecilia, Church of Santa Cecilia

Prayer in Memory of Third-Century Martyrs

Oh God, King of saints, who strengthened your servants (the martyrs) to make a good confession, staunchly resisting, for the cause of Christ, the claims of human affection, and encouraging one another in their time of trial, grant that we who cherish their blessed memory may share their pure and steadfast faith, and win with them the palm of victory; through Jesus Christ our Lord, who lives and reigns with you and the Holy Spirit, one God, for ever and ever. Amen.

(In Memory of Perpetua and Felicitas, martyred in Carthage, March 7, 203 CE)

Prayer for the Intercession of St. Cecilia

Oh gentle Cecilia, sweet voice and melody of the heart of Jesus. We come to you to beg your intercession. Pray for us, Cecilia, that we might learn through your example to sing for the glory of God, and also to sing about the glories of God. Give us the voice to sing the *Ave* as you did at the hour of your martyrdom. Pray for us oh martyr with a singing heart. Amen.

The Third-Century Roman House Below Santa Cecilia

SAN BENEDETTO

Location

San Benedetto is also in Trastevere, in fact it's in the Piazza in Piscinula just in from the Ponte Cestio as you come over across the Tiber Island. San Benedetto is actually called San Benedetto in Piscinula. The church can be hard to spot at first glance, though, since the façade is small and tucked between other buildings.

Rome

San Benedetto

The Story

According to tradition, this church is built on the site of the boyhood home of St. Benedict and his twin sister St. Scholastica. Benedict of Nursia, as he is known, was born in Nursia (modern Norcia, in Umbria, Italy) in about the year 480 CE. He lived in Rome until his late teens when he left the city to find a lifestyle that would allow him to be closer to God. He eventually became a monk, and then an abbot, founding twelve monasteries in Italy. He is most famous for creating the monastic rule that influenced all of later western monasticism. He died at Monte Cassino in 543.

The Church

While not an early worship site, San Benedetto was built around the chapel from Benedict's home, which would be from the end of the fifth century. It is also one of the best examples in Rome of a medieval church that has not lost its original look. The basilica was built in 1069, not long after the great split between the Western (Roman Catholic) church and the Eastern (Orthodox) church. The church now boasts both the oldest bell tower in Rome (eleventh century) as well as the oldest and smallest church bell in Rome.

San Benedetto, Interior

What to Look For

This church won't take very long to visit, however try to resist the temptation to get in and out quickly. Stay a while and take in the medieval feel. There is a painting of St. Benedict over the altar which some say is an actual portrait painted during his lifetime. Make sure to see the late fifth-century chapel, which can be viewed both from the portico and from the inside of the church, at the back on the left-hand side.

Prayer of St. Benedict

Gracious and holy Father, grant us the intellect to understand you, the reason to discern you, the diligence to seek you, the wisdom to find you, a spirit to know you, and a heart to meditate upon you. May our ears hear you, may our eyes see you, and may our tongues proclaim you. Give us grace that our way of life may be pleasing to you, so that we may have the patience to wait for you, and the perseverance to look for you. Grant us a

Rome

perfect end: your holy presence, a blessed resurrection, and life everlasting. We ask this through Jesus Christ our Lord. Amen.

(St. Benedict of Nursia, sixth century)

The Fifth-Century Chapel of St. Benedict, As Seen from the Portico of the Church of San Benedetto

Prayer for the Intercession of St. Benedict

Admirable saint and doctor of humility, you practiced what you taught, earnestly praying for God's glory and lovingly fulfilling all work for God and the benefit of all human beings. You know the many physical dangers that surround us today often caused or occasioned by human inventions. Guard us against poisoning of the body as well as of mind and soul, and thus be truly a "blessed one" for us. Amen.

The Fifth-Century Chapel of St. Benedict, As Seen from
Inside the Church of San Benedetto

SANTA MARIA IN TRASTEVERE (TITLE CHURCH)

Location

As the name suggests, Santa Maria in Trastevere is the last of three churches we are exploring in the region of Rome "across the Tiber." This church is west of Santa Cecilia and San Benedetto, and is best approached by going down the Via della Lungaretta, which begins at the Piazza in Piscinula. In front of the church is the Piazza Santa Maria in Trastevere, with its distinctive fountain.

The Story

There is a legend which says that in the year 38 BCE, a miraculous flow of oil sprang up on this site, which was later interpreted as a sign of the coming of Christ, though that would have happened over thirty years later. The

Rome

spot where this is supposed to have happened is now in the church and is marked by a column to the right of the altar, which bears the inscription, *Fons Olei* ("fount of oil").

Piazza Santa Maria in Trastevere

This is a title church, and according to tradition, it was a place of Christian worship going back at least to the early third century, the same general time as Santa Cecilia. There is some traditional association with bishop Callistus (217–222), who had once managed the catacombs that bear his name. Perhaps he was once the pastor of the house church on this site, and in fact archaeologists have found the remains of a Roman house beneath the baptistery.

The Churches of Rome

The Church of Santa Maria in Trastevere

The Church

The first basilica on this site was built in the fourth century (probably during the time of bishop Julius I, 337–352 CE), and was known as San Callisto in Trastevere. This building was partly destroyed in the gothic sack of Rome in 410. The church was restored by Pope Celestine in the 420s, and some time after that (probably shortly after the ecumenical Council of Ephesus in 431), it was dedicated to the Virgin Mary. It was renovated in the eighth and ninth centuries, when the remains of Popes Callistus, Julius, and Cornelius (bishop 251–253) were brought here from the tomb of the popes in the catacomb. However, most of what you see today is from the twelfth century, when the church was expanded by Pope Innocent II (1130–1143), using columns from the Baths of Caracalla. The façade is from the twelfth century, and the mosaics that you can see from the outside are from the thirteenth century. Further restoration was done in the eighteenth and nineteenth centuries, which includes the current portico, as well as the neo-Cosmati floor (just as in Santa Prassede).

Rome

Santa Maria in Trastevere, Interior

What to Look For

The mosaic in the apse is from the twelfth century, and depicts the coronation of Mary. Christ is central, and to his right and seated with him is a crowned Mary. Notice Innocent II is included presenting the church (far left), however the only ones with halos are Jesus and Mary. Peter is to the right of Jesus, but Paul is not included, and the cities of Jerusalem and Bethlehem are reversed (Bethlehem is on the right, on the same side as Peter). Where we would expect to see Paul (in this case, to the left of Mary) is the bishop Callistus. The two figures next to Peter are the bishops Cornelius and Julius. Also included in the mosaic are St. Lawrence (between Innocent and Callistus) and the third-century martyr St. Calepodius (far right).

In the chapel to the left of the altar is the ancient icon of Our Lady of Mercy, painted on wood, probably in the sixth century. It has suffered some damage over the years, including narrowly escaping a fire, but one can still see the evocative early Christian style of this painting. Also, there are two interesting paintings of the Council of Trent (1545–1563). The one that depicts the council assembly includes the personifications of Mother Church and the Virtues (the female figures in the foreground).

Before leaving the church, make sure to touch the great columns from the Baths of Caracalla. They predate the church, and are from the early third century—the very time when the first Christian congregation gathered for worship on this site.

Prayer from the Eleventh Century

We bring before you, oh God, the troubles and perils of people and nations, the sighing of prisoners and captives, the sorrows of the bereaved, the necessities of strangers, the helplessness of the weak, the despondency of the weary, the failing powers of the aged. Oh God, draw near to each, for the sake of Jesus Christ our strength. Amen.
(St. Anselm of Canterbury, eleventh century)

Santa Maria in Trastevere, Apse Mosaic

Prayer for the Intercession of Mary (Hail Holy Queen)

Hail, Holy Queen, Mother of Mercy, our life, our sweetness, and our hope.
To you do we cry, poor banished children of Eve; to you do we send up our sighs, mourning and weeping in this valley of tears. Turn then, most gracious advocate, your eyes of mercy toward us and after this our

exile show us the blessed fruit of your womb, Jesus. Oh clement, Oh loving, Oh sweet Virgin Mary.

Pray for us, Oh holy Mother of God, that we may be made worthy of the promises of Christ. Amen.

SANTA MARIA DEL POPOLO

Location

Piazza del Popolo, as Seen from Piazza Napoleone

Santa Maria del Popolo is located on the north side of Rome where several major roads converge on the Piazza del Popolo. The huge Egyptian obelisk in the piazza was one of two originally on the *spina* of the Circus Maximus. Above the Piazza, on the edge of the Villa Borghese, is the *Pincio*, a small park which includes the Piazza Napoleone. This overlook provides a spectacular view of the western side of Rome, which is well worth the steps to climb up there. Either before or after visiting the church, be sure to take in this view. If the steps are too difficult, the *Pincio* can also be approached from the upper level along the Viale Trinitá dei Monti (which turns into the Viale G. D'Annunzio) from the top of the Spanish Steps.

The Story

According to legend, the tomb of the emperor Nero (reigned 54–68 CE) was on or near this site. Nero was the first-century emperor who (probably) burned down a large portion of Rome to make room for a new palace, and then blamed the fire on the Christians. This set a precedent for persecution of the church. In addition to this, he was universally hated by the Roman people and long after his death he was infamous as the very epitome of a bad emperor. A thousand years later, as the story goes, there was a spooky old tree on the site that was home to a flock of ravens. Some people believed that the ghost of Nero roamed the area, and some even said that the ravens were demons. To combat the superstition, an early twelfth-century pope chopped down the tree and built a chapel on the site. The chapel was enlarged in the thirteenth century with donations from the people, hence the name, *del Popolo* ("of the people").

Santa Maria del Popolo

Rome

The Church

The present church is fifteenth century (Renaissance). In the seventeenth century, Bernini was put in charge of renovations and designed the current façade. The stained glass windows are the oldest in Rome.

Santa Maria del Popolo, Interior

What to Look For

The church is worth visiting as an excellent example of a Renaissance church, however the most important things to see here are two paintings by Caravaggio. In a chapel to the left of the altar are Caravaggio's *Conversion of Paul* and *Crucifixion of Peter*. They are on the side walls of the chapel, so you can't see them as you approach the chapel, but it is likely that there will be a crowd of people gathered around the chapel to see them. The *Conversion of Paul* depicts the apostle having been thrown from his horse after seeing a vision of the risen Christ (Acts 9). The *Crucifixion of Peter* shows an aging apostle being turned upside down on a cross. Both paintings are remarkable for their realism and emotion.

Prayer from the Thirteenth Century

Almighty, eternal, just and merciful God, grant us in our misery the grace to do for you alone what we know you want us to do, and always to desire what pleases you. Thus, inwardly cleansed, inwardly enlightened, and inflamed by the fire of the Holy Spirit, may we be able to follow in the footprints of your beloved Son, our Lord Jesus Christ. And by your grace alone, may we make our way to you, Most High, who live and rule in perfect Trinity and simple Unity and are glorified, God all-powerful, forever and ever. Amen.

(St. Francis of Assisi, thirteenth century)

Caravaggio's Conversion of Paul, Santa Maria del Popolo

Prayer for the Intercession of Mary, with the Hail Mary (Ave Maria)

Hail Mary, full of grace. The Lord is with you. Blessed are you among women, and blessed is the fruit of your womb, Jesus. Holy Mary, Mother of God, pray for us sinners, now and at the hour of our death. Amen.

Hail Mary, oh source of life in rebuilding salvation, you have confounded death and stepped on the serpent, to which Eve reached up stretching her neck puffed up with pride. You have trampled down that serpent in giving birth to God's Son from heaven, who was breathed into you by the Spirit of God. Hail, oh dearest and most loving mother, who have given to the world your Son sent from heaven ... Glory to the Father and the Son and the Holy Spirit. Amen.

(St. Hildegard of Bingen, twelfth century.)

Caravaggio's Crucifixion of Peter, Santa Maria del Popolo

> **Caravaggio** (c. 1572–1610)
> His real name was Michelangelo Merisi, however he is known to the world as Caravaggio, after his place of birth. Caravaggio is a transitional artist, marking the end of the Renaissance and the beginning of the Baroque period. His more famous paintings are known for their realism and their dark backgrounds, which make the characters "pop." The realism with which he chose to portray even the saints was a departure from the more symbolic representations of the past, and he was sometimes criticized for making them seem too human, even to the point of making them look dirty. It is said that he used people he found on the street, sometimes even the homeless and prostitutes, as models for his religious subjects. Constantly getting into bar fights, Caravaggio eventually had to flee Rome after killing a man. Eventually arrested, he died from a fever while in custody.
>
> Important Works of Caravaggio in Rome:
> *Conversion of Paul*—Santa Maria del Popolo
> *Crucifixion of Peter*—Santa Maria del Popolo
> *Mary and the Pilgrims* (a.k.a. *Madonna of the Pilgrims*)—Sant' Agostino
> *St. Matthew Cycle*—San Luigi dei Francesi
> *St. Francis*—Santa Maria della Concezione
> *St. Jerome*—Borghese Gallery
> *Madonna of the Serpent*—Borghese Gallery
> *John the Baptist*—Borghese Gallery
> *David with Goliath's Head*—Borghese Gallery
> *Deposition from the Cross*—Vatican Museum (Pinacoteca)

SANT' AGOSTINO

Location

Sant' Agostino is the church dedicated to St. Augustine of Hippo, the fifth-century bishop and prolific theologian from North Africa. It is located near the north end of Piazza Navona, on Piazza Sant' Agostino, near the intersection of Via della Scrofa and Via delle Coppelle. It is in the general area of the ancient title church of San Trypho, however San Trypho was torn down when Sant' Agostino was built, even though Sant' Agostino is not exactly on the same site as the earlier church.

Rome

Sant' Agostino

The Story

Before Augustine had become a bishop, in fact before he had become a Christian, he left North Africa and traveled to Rome and Milan, teaching as a professor of rhetoric. His mother had followed him, all the while praying for his conversion. She is now known to the church as St. Monica, and she is the patron saint of mothers who pray for their wayward sons. In fact, in Augustine's autobiography, *The Confessions*, Monica becomes a kind of personification of God's grace, always following, always searching to bring that lost lamb back to the fold. According to the story, when Monica arrived in Milan with her son, she complained to the bishop (St. Ambrose of Milan) that there were differences in the way the Eucharist was celebrated in North Africa, Rome, and Milan. Bishop Ambrose's answer to her was, *When in Rome, do as the Romans do*. This is said to be the origin of that expression. After Augustine's conversion and subsequent baptism by his mentor St. Ambrose, Augustine and his entourage headed back to North Africa. However, in the year 387, Monica died in the port town of Ostia before the ship could set sail from Rome. Today, one can visit the ruins of Ostia outside of

Rome. It's well worth your time, though you will need to set aside a least a half day for this excursion, and most people have not planned enough time in Rome as it is. Augustine poignantly described the loss of his mother in book nine of *The Confessions*. Monica was originally buried in Ostia, but her tomb was later moved here, to Sant' Agostino in Rome.

The Church

Another good example of a Renaissance church, Sant' Agostino (along with the adjacent monastery) was begun at the turn of the fourteenth century, but was not completed until almost 150 years later, in 1446. The stained glass windows are by the same artist as the ones in Santa Maria del Popolo, as well as Santa Maria Sopra Minerva (the only true gothic church in Rome, and also worth a visit, if you have time). The façade of Sant' Agostino was built with stone taken from the Colosseum. In 1605, the monks of the Augustinian monastery founded the Angelica Library, the oldest public library in Europe. The original church had side windows, which can still be seen from the outside, however they were completely covered up on the inside in renovations in the seventeenth century (by Borromini) and eighteenth century (by Vanvitelli, the same architect who reworked Michelangelo's design for Santa Maria degli Angeli). Further renovations were done in the nineteenth century, and completed in 1870, just in time for the new unified Italian government to confiscate the monastery and turn it into government offices. Today, most of the monastery is still occupied by the government, however a portion of it, along with the library, is left to the monks.

What to Look For

The altar was designed by Bernini, and includes as a centerpiece (above the tabernacle) an icon which is said to be from the church of Hagia Sophia (Holy Wisdom, now a mosque) in Istanbul (formerly Constantinople). The icon was probably smuggled out and brought to the west when Constantinople fell in 1453, and later surfaced when it was donated to the church in 1482. However, there are some problems with the story, not least of which is the fact that the inscription in the icon is in Latin, not Greek. Around Mary's halo are the words of the *Ave Maria* from Luke 1. Therefore some have questioned the authenticity of the icon.

Rome

Sant' Agostino, Interior

To the left of the main altar is the chapel of St. Monica, with her tomb in green marble. At the bottom of the tomb is the inscription, *S. Monica Ora Pro Nobis*, ("Saint Monica, pray for us"). Monica's body was moved here from Ostia in the fifteenth century. The tomb on the left wall is actually made up of pieces from Monica's two other tombs. You can tell that the cover does not match the sarcophagus. The sarcophagus itself is from Monica's tomb in Ostia, the cover is from the original tomb when she was brought to Rome. Notice the painting called, *The Ecstasy at Ostia*, inspired by the section in book nine of *The Confessions* in which Augustine described his last days with his mother. At one point, they are looking out a window, and Monica said she was ready to die because she had seen her son converted to the faith.

In the right transept is the Chapel of St. Augustine. Notice that in the paintings the fifth-century bishop wears the black habit of the Augustinian order, a typical device used to show the continuity between the community that Augustine started and the later order of monks. In the altar painting, Augustine is depicted with two of the first hermits: John the baptist and Paul the hermit.

On the pulpit, notice the emblem of the heart and arrow. This is a reference to a famous quote of St. Augustine, when he said (to God), "Your word has pierced my heart." In the nave you will find Raphael's painting of the prophet Isaiah, which was inspired by Michelangelo's paintings of the prophets in the Sistine Chapel. At the back of the church is the statue of Our Lady of Childbirth. Since the nineteenth century, people have left offerings and lit candles at the statue so that Mary might intercede for God's help in conception and childbirth. Notice how the foot is worn down from the hands of the many faithful who have touched the statue.

Finally, the chapel towards the back on the left holds Caravaggio's *Mary and the Pilgrims*. Notice the dark background and the realistic depiction of the pilgrims, even down to the dirt on their feet. Also notice how the baby Jesus is giving the blessing and how he is wrapped in a white cloth, symbolic of both the swaddling clothes of his birth and the shroud of his burial. Caravaggio has painted this masterpiece so that the light seems to come from Jesus and Mary. Can you identify with these pilgrims, having traveled to Rome to be closer to Jesus?

Caravaggio's Mary and the Pilgrims

Prayers of St. Augustine

We are your creatures, Lord, and we long to praise you. But we are mortal, and are reminded of our sin, and by our sin we are reminded that you humble the proud. But still we are your creation, and we want to praise you. The thought of you stirs us so deeply that we cannot be content unless we praise you, because you have made us for yourself, and our hearts are restless until they rest in you . . .

You, my God, are supreme, utmost in goodness, mightiest and all-powerful, most merciful and most just. You are the most hidden from us, and yet the most present among us, the most beautiful and yet the most powerful, ever enduring and yet we cannot comprehend you. You are unchangeable and yet you change all things. You are never new, never old, yet all things have new life from you. You are the unseen power that brings decline upon the proud. You are ever active, yet always as rest. You gather all things to yourself, though you have need of nothing. You support, you fill, and you protect all things. You create them, nourish them, and bring them to perfection . . . Amen.

(St. Augustine, adapted from book one of *The Confessions*, late fourth century)

Breathe in me, oh Holy Spirit, that my thoughts may all be holy. Act in me, oh Holy Spirit, that my work, too, may be holy. Draw my heart, oh Holy Spirit, that I love only what is holy. Strengthen me, oh Holy Spirit, to defend all that is holy. Guard me, then, oh Holy Spirit, that I always may be holy. Amen.

(St. Augustine, fifth century)

Prayer for the Intercession of St. Augustine

Holy father Augustine, saint and once a sinner, pray for us sinners. Pray that God will help us to imitate you in seeking God with all our hearts, in seeking the grace of repentance and renewal of life. Pray that God will help us to love God and neighbor at all times. Pray that God will help us to realize, as you did, that we are made for God and that our hearts will be restless, always restless, until they rest in him. Amen.

Prayer for the Intercession of St. Monica

Dear St. Monica, troubled wife and mother, many sorrows pierced your heart during your lifetime. Yet you never despaired or lost faith. With confidence, persistence, and profound faith, you prayed daily for the conversion of your beloved husband, Patricius, and your beloved son, Augustine. Your prayers were answered. Pray for me that God will grant me that same fortitude, patience, and trust in the Lord. Intercede for me, dear St. Monica, that God may favorably hear my plea for [*mention request(s)*], and grant me the grace to accept his will in all things, through Jesus Christ, our Lord, in the unity of the Holy Spirit, one God, forever and ever. Amen.

SANTA MARIA MAGGIORE (PILGRIM CHURCH, PAPAL BASILICA)

Location

Santa Maria Maggiore

Rome

Santa Maria Maggiore, or "Saint Mary Major" as it is sometimes called in English, is one of Rome's four papal basilicas, along with St. Paul Outside the Walls, St. John Lateran, and St. Peter's in the Vatican. It is located just a few blocks southwest of *Termini*, Rome's train station. It has a major piazza on both the front and back, and is the end of several major roads. The column in the Piazza Santa Maria Maggiore is originally from the Basilica of Maxentius/Constantine in the forum, though now it is topped with a bronze statue of Mary holding the baby Jesus.

The Story

According to tradition, in the fourth century there was a wealthy Christian couple who could not have children. They decided to leave their wealth to the Virgin Mary, and prayed to ask her what she would have them do with the money. Mary then appeared to them in a dream, and also to the bishop of Rome, Liberius (bishop 352–366). She told them to build a basilica, on a site which would be shown to them with a miraculous snowfall. The story goes that on August 5, in the year 358, it snowed on the Esquiline Hill in Rome. Liberius drew the outline for the new church in the snow, and to this day, August 5 is still celebrated as the feast of the Madonna of the Snow. For this reason, the church has been at times known as Santa Maria della Neve (Saint Mary of the Snow), and also as the Liberian Basilica, after the bishop.

Santa Maria Maggiore, Interior

The Church

The history of this church does go back to a fourth-century basilica, built by Liberius and dedicated in the last year of his life. In the fifth century, it was either expanded or rebuilt completely on a slightly different plan, by Pope Sixtus III (bishop 432–440). This was shortly after the third ecumenical council of Ephesus in 431, which confirmed the existing practice of calling Mary the "Mother of God." The basilica had thus become the largest church dedicated to Mary. In the seventh century, refugees from Jerusalem brought a relic of the manger of Christ, which is now under the altar, prompting the church to be called Santa Maria del Presepe (Saint Mary of the Crib). The basilica was renovated in the twelfth and thirteenth centuries (including the current floor and the portico), however parts of Sixtus' fifth-century church can still be seen. Eventually a bell tower was added in the late fourteenth century, when the papacy returned from Avignon (1377). This bell tower is still the tallest in Rome. The *baldacchino* was added and the current façade was done in the eighteenth century, and the *confessio* (under the altar) was renovated in the nineteenth century. Now the pope himself presides over Mass here every year on August 15, the Feast of the Assumption.

Santa Maria Maggiore, Apse Mosaic

Rome

What to Look For

The mosaics in and around the apse are from the thirteenth-century restoration. The earlier apse mosaic was unfortunately taken down, however its replacement is quite beautiful, depicting the coronation of Mary as Queen of Heaven. Jesus and Mary are seated, and Jesus is placing the crown on Mary's head (Rev 12:1). The inscription below them reads: "The Virgin Mary, assumed into the heavenly chamber, where the King of kings sits on a starry throne. The Holy Mother of God is elevated into the Kingdom of Heaven, above the choirs of angels." Note also just below the apse is the mosaic of the dormition of Mary, the scene of her death, where she is shown surrounded by the twelve apostles and attended by Jesus, who carries her soul to heaven where it will await the assumption of her body. Notice that Mary's soul is depicted as a smaller version of her body, in the arms of Jesus.

Santa Maria Maggiore, Left Side of the Arch Mosaic

The mosaics on the triumphal arch, along with some in the nave, are from Sixtus' fifth-century basilica (note the inscription on the arch with Sixtus' name in it—it says: "Sixtus, Bishop of the People"). Though they are damaged (cut off on both sides), the mosaics of the arch commemorate the third ecumenical council of Ephesus in 431, and show scenes of the life of Mary and the infant Jesus. On the left side of the arch are the scenes of the annunciation, the angel visitation to Joseph, the adoration of the magi (the third magus is missing), and the slaughter of the innocents, along with the city of Jerusalem. On the right side we see the presentation of Jesus in the temple, the Holy Family's flight into Egypt (including a legend about Egyptian idols falling over), the magi with Herod, and the city of Bethlehem. In the center is the throne of the Book

Santa Maria Maggiore, Right Side of the Arch Mosaic

of Revelation with the seven seals and the winged symbols of the four evangelists. On either side of the throne are the apostles Peter (on the left) and Paul (on the right). Although the position of the apostles is the reverse of what we would expect from such an early mosaic, the cities of Jerusalem and Bethlehem are also reversed, so that Peter is still on the same side as Jerusalem and Paul is on the same side as Bethlehem. Here it is clear that keeping the two apostles with their symbolic cities was more important than keeping them on their traditional sides, and in fact their reversal may reflect the growing primacy of Peter as the predecessor to the bishops of Rome. In other words, now Peter, not Paul, is at the right hand of the throne of Jesus.

Along the walls above the pillars in the nave are several ancient mosaics from the fifth-century basilica, or as some believe, possibly even from the fourth-century Liberian church. They depict scenes from the Old Testament, as well as the annunciation and the adoration of the magi, however almost half of them did not survive the centuries and have been replaced with painted copies.

The remains of St. Matthias are entombed in the altar. Below the main altar is the relic of the manger, said to have been venerated in the Holy Land until it was smuggled out during the Arab conquests. According to tradition it was brought to Rome and given to Pope Theodore I (bishop 642–649), along with the remains of St. Jerome, whose tomb is now also under the altar. The relic of the manger is kept in a vault that closes at the end of the day, so don't expect to visit Santa Maria Maggiore near closing time, or you might miss it. Facing the relic of the manger is the larger-than-life statue of Pope Pius IX, who was responsible for renovating the so-called Bethlehem Crypt under the altar in the nineteenth century. Pius IX was also the pope who clarified the dogma of the Immaculate Conception of Mary (1854) and the concept of *ex cathedra* papal infallibility (1870).

On the right side of the chancel (you might have to look for it) is the tomb of Bernini. It is under the floor, and only marked with an inlaid inscription, which says, "Here the noble Bernini family awaits the resurrection."

The so-called Sistine Chapel is named after the tomb of Sixtus V (bishop 1521–1590). It contains the Crypt of the Crèche, with a reliquary below the chapel altar containing pieces of an ancient nativity scene that was here until it was accidentally broken when the Sistine Chapel was being built.

The Pauline Chapel, also called the Borghese Chapel, has as its altarpiece an icon of Mary, one of several paintings in Italy that claim to be the *Madonna di San Luca* (Madonna of St. Luke), an actual portrait of Mary painted by the apostle Luke, who is said to have been an artist as well as a physician. It is also called the *Salus Populi Romani* (meaning salvation, or healing, of the Roman people). It is called this because it is said to have saved the people of Rome when it was processed through the streets during times of great tragedy. There are legends that an icon of Mary was processed through the streets, encouraging the prayers of the people, which led to the end of the plague during the time of Gregory the Great (see above, under Castel Sant' Angelo), as well as at least one medieval plague. There is also a story that in the ninth century, Pope Leo IV (bishop 847–855) processed an icon of Mary through the neighborhood of the Borgo (adjacent to the Vatican) to put out a huge fire there (see above, under Vatican Museums for the painting *Fire in the Borgo*, in which you can see the façade of the old St. Peter's basilica). However, this particular icon was probably painted in the thirteenth century.

Above the icon is a relief sculpture of Pope Liberius tracing the outline of the basilica in the snow (it looks like he's using a hoe). This is by Stefano Maderno (1576–1636), the same sculptor who created the statue of the body of St. Cecilia. The Pauline Chapel is now used as a Eucharistic adoration chapel, so you will probably have to view the altar and icon from the doorway.

The baptistery is mostly from the Renaissance, however the relief above the altar is *The Assumption of the Virgin*, by Pietro Bernini, father of the more famous Gian Lorenzo Bernini. Look for the bust of Antonio Emanuele Ne Vunda, the ambassador of Congo, who died while in Rome for an audience with Pope Paul V in 1608. The bust is made from an actual death mask, though his outfit is probably more symbolic than historically accurate.

Along one of the side aisles you will find the statue of Mary known as the *Regina Pacis* (Queen of Peace). This statue commemorates the end of World War I—note Mary's hand in the "stop" position. At her feet is a dove, and Jesus holds an olive branch, both symbols of peace.

The circle on the floor in the nave is said to mark the spot where the wealthy couple who originally donated the money for the first church on this site were buried. Their remains are now said to be in the altar with St. Matthias. Also notice the crest of the Borghese family (the eagle and dragon) in the floor. Pope Paul V (bishop 1552–1621), whose tomb is here, was of the Borghese family, the same family that gave its name to the "Central Park" of Rome, the Villa Borghese.

The Regina Pacis, Santa Maria Maggiore

Now look up. The gold on the ceiling was donated to Pope Alexander VI (Borgia, bishop 1492–1503) by Ferdinand and Isabella of Spain, and according to tradition, was from the first shipment of gold to come back from the Americas (probably Peru). The Borgia crest can be seen in the ceiling.

Since this is one of the four papal basilicas, it has a Holy Door (*Porta Santa*). This one was dedicated and blessed by Pope John Paul II. It has relief sculptures of the Council of Ephesus (bottom left) and the Second Vatican Council (bottom right). Above the images of Mary and Jesus are the two titles of Mary, Mother of God and Mother of the Church (Rev 12:17).

There is a museum below the basilica, which contains some interesting (but dubious) relics of the evangelists, as well as the remains of an ancient Roman wall. The museum is frankly not a "must see," but is more of a curiosity if one has extra time. To enter the museum, ask at the gift shop.

Before leaving, try to see the outdoor mosaic behind the eighteenth-century façade. It shows Pope Liberius and the wealthy but childless couple being shown where to build the church.

Prayer from the Twelfth Century

Oh fire of the Helping Spirit, the life of every creature's life, you are holy in giving life to forms. You are holy in anointing the severely injured, holy in cleansing foul wounds. Oh breath of holiness, fire of love, oh sweet taste in our bodies and pouring in our hearts of the fragrance of all virtues. Oh clearest fountain, in which is shown how God gathers together those who wander and seeks those who are lost . . . Let there be praise to you who are the sound of all praise and the joy of life, who are hope and powerful honor, granting the gifts of light. Amen.

(St. Hildegard of Bingen, twelfth century)

Ancient Prayer for the Intercession of Mary "Theotokos" (Mother of God)

Oh most glorious Ever-Virgin Mary, Mother of Christ our God, accept our prayers and present them to your Son and our God, that he may, for your sake, enlighten and save our souls . . . [*mention request(s)*]

Oh may I obtain this, most holy lady and Mother of God, through your intercessions and mediations, by the grace and exceeding great love of your only-begotten Son, my Lord and God and Savior, Jesus Christ, to whom is due, with the eternal Father and the all-holy, good and life-giving Spirit, all honor and glory and worship, now and forever, and into eternity. Amen.

SAN PAOLO FUORI LE MURA (PILGRIM CHURCH, PAPAL BASILICA)

Location

St. Paul Outside the Walls is located on the south end of Rome, along the Via Ostiense. It would be a long walk to get there, but there is a metro station (San Paolo station) close by. When you come out of the metro station, you have to cross the major street (Via Ostiense) and then go around to the front of the basilica, which is on the Viale di San Paolo.

San Paolo Fuori le Mura

The Story

This church is built on the site of the tomb of the apostle Paul. Since Paul was a Roman citizen, he was beheaded, rather than crucified as Peter was. Beheading was considered a more merciful execution because it was quicker. Still, all executions had to be done outside of the city walls. While there are some conflicting accounts that also link this site with Paul's death, the more likely site of his martyrdom is at a different site, called the *Tre Fontane* (Three Fountains), where legend says that when Paul was beheaded, his head bounced three times, and a spring miraculously bubbled up from each of the three places where his head hit the ground. At Tre Fontane, there are three churches, and one of them is built around three springs, however the springs were already known in Roman literary sources before the time when Paul was beheaded, and in fact they are probably too far apart for a human head to bounce from one spot to the next. In any case, if we assume that Paul was beheaded in the area of Tre Fontane, he was then buried here along the road to Ostia. As I have mentioned above, there is also a tradition that says that the bodies of both Peter and Paul were moved temporarily to the catacombs of San Sebastiano. If this tradition is true, then at some time when the persecution subsided, their bodies were returned to the sites of their respective tombs, and Paul's remains were brought back here. His tomb is still directly under the main altar.

The Church

The emperor Constantine built a martyrium over the tomb of Paul, which was consecrated by bishop Sylvester I in 324 CE. This was originally a small chapel or shrine with the apse on the west end, and the main entrance facing the road. It probably did not hold more than a few hundred people at one time. The original tomb marker had access holes so that people could drop in an offering, or reach in with a handkerchief or other personal item and touch the tomb. In fact, archaeologists have found coins from all over the world that were dropped into the access holes. However, the martyrium very quickly became such a popular site for pilgrims to visit that the traffic of faithful outgrew the space. Eventually, the chapel had to be enlarged, but because the tomb of Paul was so close to the road, the orientation of the church was reversed, so that the main altar would still be directly above the tomb, but the nave could be much bigger. This is why today the entrance to the church is on the side away from the main road. The basilica was commissioned by the emperor Theodosius (reigned 346–395), who justified the reversal of orientation by saying that it symbolized Paul's mission to the Gentiles—facing west, rather than east. The new basilica was consecrated by Pope Siricius (bishop 384–399) in the year 390, but was not actually completed until 395, shortly after the emperor Theodosius died. Care of the church was entrusted to the Benedictines in the eighth century, and it remains a Benedictine church, which is why it includes a chapel dedicated to Benedict, with an imposing statue of the saint.

Since this church is outside the walls, it was vulnerable to attack by ransacking invaders. This happened in the eighth century (the Lombards) and in the ninth century (the Arabs), and most of the treasures of the original basilica were taken. This prompted Pope John VIII (bishop

872–882) to build a protection wall around the area, just as Leo IV had done around the Vatican a few decades before. The campus of the basilica came to be called "Johnstown" (*Johannipolis*), and the walls successfully protected the church from the German invasion in 1084.

The basilica remained in this state until it was destroyed by a fire in 1823. Rebuilding began immediately, with gifts from all over the world, including exotic marbles and precious stones from Egypt and Russia. In spite of the fact that it was almost completely built new in the nineteenth century, the church still retains the size, the basic plan, and much of the feel of the ancient basilica. As the second largest church in Rome (after St. Peter's in the Vatican), Saint Paul Outside the Walls is a successful balance of grandeur without unnecessary opulence. The new church was dedicated on December 10, 1854 by Pope Pius IX, who had confirmed the dogma of the Immaculate Conception just two days earlier. Thus, this church has some association with that event, and includes six large ornamental documents (three on each side of the papal throne) that list the names of the bishops who were present for the two events. Note also that the column in Piazza di Spagna (near the foot of the Spanish Steps) was dedicated to the Immaculate Conception, and the inscription on the base of the column contains the words of the Hail Mary prayer, from Luke 1:28, 42.

San Paolo Fuori le Mura, Interior

Although most of what you will see in San Paolo dates from the nineteenth century, some important elements remain from the earlier basilica, including the apse mosaic and the cloister, both from the thirteenth century.

What to Look For

As you approach the basilica, you will no doubt get a sense of the grandeur of the place before you even enter. The beautiful courtyard has at its center a huge statue of Paul with a sword, both the method of his martyrdom as well as a metaphor for the Scriptures (Eph 6:17), his contribution to which is symbolized by the book he holds in his other hand. Behind Paul off to the right is a statue of Luke, Paul's disciple and chronicler. Statues of Peter and Paul also flank the doors. On the tympanum (upper register) of the façade is a nineteenth-century mosaic. Notice Jesus in the center, on a throne, with Peter on the left (at Jesus' right hand) and Paul on the right. Here, even on the church dedicated to Paul, the apostle to the Gentiles defers the place of greater honor to Peter, the predecessor of the bishops of Rome. Notice the Lamb of God with the four rivers of paradise, and the lambs coming from Jerusalem and Bethlehem, although now with a more modern (realistic) look. Below the Lamb of God are the four prophets Isaiah, Jeremiah, Ezekiel, and Daniel, all of whom predicted the coming of the Messiah. This mosaic replaced a thirteenth-century mosaic from the original façade—the surviving fragments of the earlier one are now on the reverse side of the triumphal arch over the altar.

The central door is decorated with a twentieth-century relief sculpture of a cross as the tree of life. It also contains scenes from the lives of Peter and Paul. Note that the figure of Jesus stands out in silver. On the right, he confronts Paul on the road to Damascus (Acts 9); and on the left, he gives Peter the keys of the kingdom (Matthew 16). The Holy Door, created for the year 2000 jubilee, shows Pope John Paul II gathering the poor and the sick in front of St. Peter's basilica.

As you enter the nave, note that the floor is not the original floor, it was elevated in the rebuilding, however some of the tombs that made up the original floor can still be seen through glass in the floor along the right-hand side. From the inside, take a look at the back side of the Holy Door—this is actually the old central door from the original basilica. This door came from Constantinople, not long after the great split between the Western (Roman Catholic) and Eastern (Orthodox) halves of the church. The door was commissioned in the year 1070 by a wealthy merchant, and given as a penance for his role in slave trade. It was presented to the abbot of the church, who in 1073 would become Pope Gregory VII (Hildebrand).

The mosaics on the triumphal arch were originally done in the fifth century (contemporary with the oldest mosaics in Santa Maria Maggiore), though they were heavily restored in the nineteenth century. Along the top we can see the four winged creatures of the Book of Revelation, surrounding a particularly unflattering picture of Jesus with the rod of judgment, and below that are the twenty-four white-robed elders (Rev 4:4), twelve on each side, presented as martyrs with their crowns. Beneath the elders/martyrs are the apostles: Paul is on the left, pointing to his tomb, and Peter is on the right. However the statues in front of the arch are the reverse of this, with Peter on the left and Paul on the right. On the ceiling is the coat of arms of Pope Pius IX.

San Paolo Fuori le Mura, Apse Mosaic

The apse mosaic is from the thirteenth century, though it too had to be somewhat restored after the fire. In the center is Jesus seated, with his hand upheld in blessing. The position of his hand is meant to convey both the three-in-one of the Trinity, as well as the two-in-one of the person of Christ (both human and divine). In his other hand, he is holding a book which says in Latin: "Come, you blessed of my Father, receive the Kingdom that has been prepared for you since the foundation of the world" (Matt 25:34). Paul is on the left (on Jesus' right) holding a scroll that says: "At the name of Jesus, let every knee bow down, in heaven, on earth and under the earth" (from Paul's letter to the Philippians 2:10). Here Paul holds the place of higher honor, and only Paul's name is written in both Latin and Greek (on both sides of his head). Peter is on the right, holding a scroll which contains the words of his confession of faith from the gospel: "You are the Christ, the Son of the Living God" (Matt 16:16). The other apostles represented are Luke (next to Paul) and Andrew (next to Peter).

You may notice what looks like a little baby at Jesus' feet. That is actually Pope Honorius III, who was bishop of Rome when this mosaic was made (1216–1227). Rather than place himself alongside the apostles and saints but with a square halo, he had himself depicted very small, kissing Jesus' foot. The lower scene shows the apostles waiting around an empty throne—this is the throne of judgment that awaits the coming of the Judge. In Greek this image is referred to as the *Hetoimasia*, meaning "preparation." Around the throne are the instruments of Christ's passion: the cross, the crown of thorns, the spear, nails, and a sponge.

Beneath the mosaic in the apse is a papal throne (*cathedra*). Since this is one of the four papal basilicas, its altar is one of the papal altars, where the pope himself may preside over the Eucharist. The relief sculpture on the throne shows Christ giving Peter the keys of the kingdom. The *baldacchino* is also from the thirteenth century, and is a rare example of gothic architecture in Rome. On the back side of the triumphal arch are those fragments of the medieval façade mosaic that survive.

In the altar are the chains which are said to have held Paul when he was under arrest in Rome (Acts 28). Beneath the altar is the tomb of Paul. This is the same place that has been venerated as the tomb of Paul since before the fourth century, and in fact there is a tomb marker naming Paul that dates from the time of Constantine's martyrium. This is the one that contains the access holes for the early pilgrims to touch the tomb or leave an offering (it is now in the museum off the cloister, hanging high on the wall). Today, you can see the tomb from the front through a metal grate, and you can actually see Paul's sarcophagus. You can also see through a glass section in the floor and get a glimpse of part of the Constantinian

Rome

martyrium that was first built to honor the apostle's tomb. As you look down at this, you are seeing part of the original apse, since the church faced the opposite way.

The elaborate candlestick for the Easter candle is from the twelfth century. If you look close in the reliefs you may find an image of Pontius Pilate in a *mandorla* (full body halo), based on a legend that he converted to Christianity after Christ's resurrection.

The church is decorated with frescoes showing scenes from the story of Paul in the book of Acts. It is also decorated with gifts from around the world, which came in after the fire when the church was being rebuilt. The two green side altars are made of malachite and lapis lazuli, gifts of Czar Nicholas I of Russia. These are in the chapels of The Conversion of St. Paul and The Assumption of the Blessed Virgin. A series of windows made of thin sheets of alabaster, which cast a warm light on the nave, were a gift from the king of Egypt, along with the six alabaster columns on the inside of the front wall of the basilica.

The Cloister, San Paolo Fuori le Mura

One feature for which this church is famous, is the series of portraits of the popes around the perimeter. This was a tradition begun in the fifth century by Pope Leo I (Leo the Great, bishop 440–461). The originals were frescoes, painted on the plaster, but only forty-one of them survived the fire, and they are now in the abbey. The present ones are mosaic copies, but of course we cannot assume that they are the actual likenesses of the early popes. Notice that there is a spotlight on the current pope, and that there are spaces left for future popes.

The altar of the baptistery is one of the altars from the original basilica. It holds the remains of St. Timothy of Antioch (martyred in 311 CE), as well as some other martyrs. The marble in the baptistery is from all over the world and is meant to represent the Christians who come from all over the world, as well as the worldwide nature of the one baptism of the faith.

Be sure to visit the thirteenth-century cloister, which is one of the few remaining (beautifully preserved) medieval cloisters. It is a wonderful place to stop and reflect, while viewing all of the ancient artifacts around the perimeter as well as the garden in the middle. There is also a museum attached to the cloister, which contains some medieval documents, vestments, reliquaries, and other religious articles, including a ninth-century Bible (the Charles the Bald Bible).

Prayer of St. Paul

God of our Lord Jesus Christ, Father of Glory, give us a spirit of wisdom and revelation so that we may understand you better. Illuminate the eyes of our hearts so that we may know the hope of your calling, the richness of your glory, and the inheritance of your saints . . . Fill us with the knowledge of your will through all spiritual wisdom and understanding so that we may live in a manner worthy of our Lord, to be more fully pleasing to you, bearing fruit and growing in the knowledge of you. Strengthen us with power according to your glorious might, for all endurance and patience. With joy, we give thanks to you, Father, for making us fit to share in the inheritance of the saints in light, for delivering us from the power of darkness and transferring us to the Kingdom of your beloved Son, in whom we have redemption through the forgiveness of our sins. Amen.

(St. Paul, adapted from his letters to the Ephesians and Colossians, first century)

Prayer for the Intercession of St. Paul

Oh glorious Saint Paul, after persecuting the church you became by God's grace its most zealous apostle. To carry the knowledge of Jesus, our divine Savior, to the uttermost parts of the earth you joyfully endured prison, scourgings, stonings, and shipwreck, as well as all manner of persecutions culminating in the shedding of the last drop of your blood for our Lord Jesus Christ.

    Pray for us the grace to labor strenuously to bring the faith to others and to accept any trials and tribulations that may come our way. Pray for us to be inspired by your epistles and to share in your unyielding love for Jesus, so that after we have finished our course we may join you in praising him in heaven for all eternity. Amen.

SAN GIOVANNI IN LATERANO (PILGRIM CHURCH, PAPAL BASILICA, CATHEDRAL OF ROME)

Location

One might assume that St. Peter's in the Vatican is the cathedral of Rome, however it is not. The word "cathedral" has nothing to do with the size or architecture of a church. Rather it indicates the church of the *cathedra* or "chair" of the bishop. Therefore, the cathedral is the bishop's church. But since the bishop of Rome is the pope, that still might lead us to think that St. Peter's must be the cathedral. However, officially the seat of the bishop of Rome has always been San Giovanni in Laterano, or St. John Lateran. San Giovanni is located along the southeastern part of the city walls, somewhat between the Colosseum and Santa Croce in Gerusalemme. It is the end of the Via di San Giovanni in Laterano. The area of the cathedral includes the basilica itself, as well as the ancient baptistery, San Giovanni in Fonte, and the Holy Stairs (Santa Scala). These two latter sites are not always open all day, so it's a good idea to try to visit the cathedral in the morning and go to the baptistery first.

    The obelisk in the piazza is the oldest in Rome (about 3,500 years old), created in the fifteenth century BCE. It was taken from Egypt by the emperor Constantine, who meant for it to be used in the building of his new city Constantinople, however it only got as far as the mouth of the Nile before Constantine died. It sat in Alexandria for years until it was brought to Rome by one of the sons of Constantine in the year 357. It was originally

The Churches of Rome

placed on the *spina* of the Circus Maximus, however it was eventually toppled (probably during a barbarian invasion) and lay broken in three pieces until it was buried by debris. It was found in the ruins of the Circus in the year 1587, and in 1588 Pope Sixtus V (bishop 1585–1590) had it dug up, repaired, and moved to the Lateran basilica. Even though small sections had to be removed in order to repair it, it remains the tallest (over one hundred feet) of all the Egyptian obelisks in Rome. It was topped with a cross, as a symbol of the victory of Christianity over paganism.

The Cathedral of Rome, San Giovanni in Laterano

The Story

This church is not built on the site of an ancient house church or martyr's tomb. In fact, it is built on the foundations of the barracks of the Augustan Cavalry, an elite squad of equestrians who were meant to be the emperor's bodyguard. While there are various conflicting stories, the name *Laterani* seems to come from the original owners of the land, the Laterani family, who had a mansion adjacent to the barracks. It appears that the emperor Nero confiscated the land from the Laterani after charging a member of the family with treason and having him executed. In any

Rome

event, by the third century, the land was in the hands of the emperors, who apparently used the mansion as a safehouse in close proximity to the cavalry. When Maxentius occupied Rome in the early fourth century, this was his headquarters, and the cavalry fought for him against Constantine. When Constantine entered the city after the Battle at the Milvian Bridge (and the death of Maxentius) on October 28, 312, he took possession of the Lateran estate, and stayed there while he remained in Rome. Another version of the story says that Constantine acquired the land as part of a dowry when he married Maxentius' sister Fausta before they went to war against each other (this Fausta would later be caught as a ringleader in a plot against Constantine's life and executed). Eventually Constantine gave the land to Bishop Miltiades (bishop 311–314) to be used for a new basilica. The cavalry barracks would become the foundation for the new church, while the private grotto (a *nymphaeum*, like an indoor garden with a fountain) would become the first free-standing baptistery in Rome, and the mansion would become the residence of the bishops of Rome—the first papal apartments.

There is a legend that says that when Jerusalem was sacked in the year 70 CE, the general and future emperor Titus brought the spoils of war back to Rome (which can be seen on the Arch of Titus), and that these spoils included the biblical ark of the covenant. The treasures were either housed in the Forum of Peace (Vespasian), under what is now the church of Santi Cosma e Damiano, or they were brought directly to the Lateran palace. If they were originally in the Forum of Peace, then they were later brought to the Lateran when it became the cathedral of Rome. Either way, the legend suggests that the ark of the covenant was once kept in San Giovanni. This legend goes on to say that it was taken during a barbarian invasion in the year 455, and ended up in Carthage, in North Africa. There it was recaptured by Christian soldiers of the Eastern empire, and taken to Constantinople. From there it was meant to be sent back to Jerusalem, but was lost at sea when the ship carrying it sank in the Mediterranean.

The Church

San Giovanni was one of the first of the basilicas commissioned (and paid for) by the emperor Constantine after the legalization of Christianity. Built in 324, it was patterned after the great basilicas of the forum, and held about 3,500 people. As far as we know it was originally dedicated to John the Baptist. After barbarian Vandals ransacked the church and stole its treasures in 455 CE, it was restored by Pope Leo I (Leo the Great, bishop 440–461). The bishops' residence was enlarged to become a palace in the eighth century. However the complex was heavily damaged by an earthquake in the ninth century. The basilica was completely redone in the twelfth century, when the dedication to St. John the Apostle was added, so that now the church is dedicated to both Johns.

Five major councils, known as the Lateran Councils, were held here, in 1123, 1139, 1179, 1215, and 1515. Kings and emperors were crowned here by the medieval popes (though not Charlemagne, he was crowned in the old St. Peter's basilica). This is where St. Francis met Pope Innocent III to receive permission to found the order of the Franciscans. Note the statue of Francis in the park near the Porta San Giovanni. The bishops of Rome lived in the Lateran residence until the papacy was removed to Avignon in 1309.

The church was damaged by fire in the fourteenth century, which some said was God's punishment for taking the papacy to Avignon. The French popes did allocate money to rebuild after the fire, but by the time Gregory XI brought the papacy back to Rome in 1377, the church was in bad shape, and the residence was no longer livable. Gregory went to live in the Vatican, which became the papal residence, as it remains today. (There was a span time from the late sixteenth century to 1870, when the popes lived in the Quirinal Palace. However, in 1870, the Quirinal Palace was confiscated by the new Italian government, along with the friary at Sant' Agostino. Today the Quirinal Palace is the "White House" of Italy, home to its president.)

Repairs of the fire damage were not complete until the fifteenth century, when marble was taken from the Colosseum to finish the work. More restoration was done in the sixteenth century under Sixtus V, however what you see today is mostly the work of a renovation designed by Borromini in the seventeenth century. It was commissioned by Pope Innocent X (bishop 1644–1655) for the 1650 jubilee. Thankfully, Borromini was prevented by the pope from making all the changes he wanted, and so some of the older elements of the basilica were preserved. The façade was done in the eighteenth century, and it is from the balcony of San Giovanni that the pope gives his annual Holy Thursday blessing.

Rome

In the year 1929, the Lateran Treaty was signed here, which made the Vatican a sovereign state, but stipulated that the other three papal basilicas outside the Vatican are also part of the Vatican's domain.

San Giovanni in Fonte

The baptistery is a small, separate building that now feels like it's out in the parking lot. If you approach the cathedral from Via di San Giovanni in Laterano (you may be coming from the Colosseum and/or San Clemente), you will come to the baptistery first. It was built by the emperor Constantine even before the church, possibly as early as the year 315. Since the cathedral is the bishop's church, and baptism was originally only done by the bishops, it is natural that the cathedral should be the one church with a baptistery. Anyone who got baptized in Rome in the fourth century was probably baptized here at Easter. San Giovanni in Fonte was not just the baptistery of this basilica, it was the baptistery of Rome, and it is possible that the fact that this was *the* place of baptism in Rome prompted the dedication of the whole cathedral to John the Baptist. Perhaps the cathedral was called San Giovanni simply because the baptistery already was.

San Giovanni in Fonte, the Baptistery at San Giovanni in Laterano

The Churches of Rome

The building was originally round and would have resembled Santa Costanza, the mausoleum built by Constantine for his daughter. However the octagonal exterior and much of what you will see is from a remodeling done in the fifth century by Pope Sixtus III (bishop 432–440). With the legalization of Christianity, the church of Rome grew exponentially, and so eventually there were too many baptisms to be held in one place (or indeed at only one time of year) and other churches began to have their own baptisteries. Thus the concept of a free-standing baptistery was short lived.

According to literary sources, the original font was of red porphyry marble, with a thirty-pound golden lamb and seven eighty-pound silver deer, all pouring water into it. In the middle of the font was a fifty-pound candle, and on either side were silver statues of Jesus and John the Baptist. Imagine that there would have been curtains hanging from the inner row of columns around the central area, for privacy. In the early church, people were baptized in the nude (women attended by deaconesses), and clothed with a new white robe upon coming out of the water.

The Original Floor of the Lateran Nymphaeum, as Seen Below the St. Venantius Chapel of San Giovanni in Fonte

Rome

The smaller side chapels were added to the baptistery in the late fifth century. One has a fifth-century apse mosaic with a tree of life motif on a dark blue background. The Chapel of St. John the evangelist includes a Lamb of God with the victory wreath of resurrection. The largest chapel was added in the seventh century, however you can see exposed below the floor is the original (pre-fourth century) floor of the Lateran *nymphaeum*. This chapel is dedicated to St. Venantius (also known as St. Wigand), a bishop of Salona who was martyred in the early fourth century. His remains, along with those of his predecessor and fellow martyr St. Domnio, were brought to Rome in 640 by Pope John IV (bishop 640–642). The chapel was created to house their relics, along with some of the first martyrs' relics to be brought into the city from the catacombs. In the seventh-century mosaic, Pope John IV holds a model of the chapel. The martyrs depicted are some of those whose remains were brought here, including the Saints Venantius and Domnio.

The St. Venantius Chapel of San Giovanni in Fonte

Santa Scala (Holy Stairs)

On the opposite side of the basilica, in another separate building across a street, is the staircase, said to be from the so-called *Praetorium* in

Jerusalem. The word "praetorium" implies the headquarters of the Praetorian Guard, the elite guard of the Roman emperors. However in the provinces, the word came to be used for the headquarters of whatever Roman official was in charge of the local legions. In Jerusalem, this would have been the palace of Herod, which after Judea became a Roman colony, was used by Pontius Pilate whenever he was in town. The building is mentioned in the gospels as the place where Jesus was taken to face Pontius Pilate (Matt 27:27; Mark 15:16; John 18:28-40; 19:9). Thus these stairs are believed to be those which Jesus ascended to be sentenced to die. They are sometimes called the *Scala Pilati*, the Stairs of Pilate. According to tradition, the Jerusalem palace was identified by Constantine's mother Helena and the stairs were brought back to Rome in 362 CE. They were given to Pope Sylvester, who had them built into the original cathedral. They were moved in 1589, and now they lead up to the *Sancta Sanctorum*, the private chapel of the early popes, and the sole surviving room of the original papal apartments. The altar of this ancient chapel is said to contain some of the oldest relics of the church, collected and placed there by Pope Leo III in the eighth century, though the mystique surrounding this place has given rise to some fanciful rumors, including that the cache of relics once included the heads of Peter and Paul. The relics of countless unnamed martyrs, whose remains were removed from the catacombs, are said to be under the stairs.

The pilgrim traffic of so many centuries had begun to wear the marble down, so they were eventually covered with wooden steps, however holes were left in the front of the steps so that the faithful could put a hand in and touch the marble where Jesus walked. There are also small windows in the wooden stairs, now obscured by age and no longer transparent, but it is said that once upon a time, one could look down onto the marble and see stains of Jesus' blood. Today, no one walks up the stairs. The only way to ascend the holy stairs is on your knees, and doing so is considered a form of penance. Pope Gregory VII seems to have started this tradition, which was followed by (among many others) Pope Pius IX in 1870, on the eve of the invasion of Rome that resulted in the unification of Italy.

Whether you choose to ascend the stairs on your knees or not, take a moment to at least kneel on the first step, and touch the marble through the slot in the front. Of all the holy relics brought back from Jerusalem, this set of stairs has a high degree of probability, since it would not be hard to identify the Herodian palace where Pilate stayed during Passover of 33 CE and where Jesus was brought to be sentenced.

The Leonine Triclinium, Part of the Original Papal Apartments at San Giovanni in Laterano

Before leaving the Santa Scala, notice the large outdoor apse around the corner of the building. This is a fragment of the old Lateran palace, what had become the *Triclinium Leoninum*, the papal dining hall of Leo III (bishop 795–816). Leo III was the pope who crowned Charlemagne Holy Roman Emperor in the year 800. The mosaic is from this time, and commemorates the event. Note the two groups on the arch of the apse. On the left is Christ giving the keys of the kingdom to Peter, and giving a banner to the emperor Constantine. On the right is Peter (keys in his lap) with Pope Leo III and Charlemagne, both of whom have square halos. The *triclinium* (dining hall) was torn down in the sixteenth century, so that only this apse remains, however it was preserved by turning it into a kind of monument. Today the only remnants of the original Lateran palace are the *Sancta Sanctorum* chapel at the top of the Holy Stairs and the *triclinium* apse.

The Cathedral

The inscription on the eighteenth-century façade of the catheral says, "The sacred Lateran church, mother and head of all churches in the city and in the world." This is a reference to a papal pronouncement of 1372 declaring San Giovanni the primary church of Christendom. The text of the pronouncement is preserved in a marble plaque inside the basilica. It is interesting to note that the papacy was still in Avignon when this pronouncement was issued but would return to Rome five years later.

The Cathedral of Rome, San Giovanni in Laterano, Interior

What to Look For

The main doors of the church, though normally closed, are the massive bronze doors from the *Curia* in the forum, and date back to the fourth century. Thankfully, Borromini was prevented from replacing them, along with the fourteenth-century gothic *baldacchino*, a gift of king Charles V of France. You may enter the basilica through the smaller doors, or through the secondary façade on the side nearest the baptistery. Either way, don't miss the two interesting statues in the porticos. Just inside the main façade is the fourth-century statue of the emperor Constantine. In the other portico on the baptistery side is a statue of Charlemagne, posing in a similar position. This statue of Charlemagne, and that fact that it is here at the cathedral opposite the statue of Constantine, is probably meant as a form of propaganda - to convey the idea that Charlemagne was a new Constantine, uniting Europe under the banner of Christ, as Constantine had done for the Roman empire.

Fourth-Century Statue of the Emperor Constantine, San Giovanni in Laterano

The apse mosaic is probably originally from the eighth century, however it was heavily reworked in the year 1290 by Pope Nicholas IV (bishop 1288–1292), who had himself added to the scene. He is shown smaller than the rest, kneeling next to Mary, whose hand is on his head in a gesture of protection. The mosaic was restored again in the nineteenth century, by order of Pope Pius IX. Notice that it is not Jesus who is central, but the cross, though Jesus is depicted in heaven in the center above the cross. To the left of the cross is Mary, while the apostles Peter and Paul are on the far left. On the other side are the two Johns, with Andrew on the far right. The cross is ornate, rather like the cross in the apse of Santa Pudenziana, and does not have the body of Jesus on it, which may indicate that this is the oldest part of the mosaic. Directly beneath the cross is the phoenix in a palm tree, symbols of resurrection and eternal life. The cross is on the familiar hill from which flow the four rivers of paradise, however here the cross is also bathed in the living water which is shown coming from the Holy Spirit (depicted as a dove). All of the water flows into the Jordan River, which runs across the front of the scene just below everyone's feet. St. Francis is shown (between Mary and Peter), smaller than the apostles but larger than the pope (who was a Franciscan). St. Anthony is also depicted the same size as St. Francis.

San Giovanni in Laterano, Apse Mosaic

The tomb under the altar is that of Pope Martin V (bishop 1417–1431), who finally restored the church after the return of the papacy from Avignon. Above the altar, in the *baldacchino*, is a part of the table said to be the first "papal altar," where Peter himself presided over the Eucharist (at Santa Pudenziana). According to tradition, this table continued to be used as a Eucharistic altar by all of the bishops of Rome until the time when Constantine began building the first basilicas.

In the left transept is the altar of the Holy Sacrament. The large bronze columns were taken from the temple of Jupiter that was once on the Capitoline Hill (the foundation walls are in the Capitoline Museum), and the bronze itself had once been part of Cleopatra's ships, taken after she and Marc Antony lost the Battle of Actium in 31 BCE. Above the altar is the relic of the Holy Table, a fragment of wood said to be part of the table on which Jesus and his disciples shared the Last Supper, and on which he instituted the sacrament of the Lord's Supper.

Look for the paintings on legendary events from the life of the emperor Constantine. One shows the baptism of Constantine by Sylvester of Rome (bishop 314–335). This never happened but is based on a medieval legend that says Constantine had contracted leprosy and was told by Peter and Paul in a dream to be baptized, and then he was cured. In reality, Constantine was not baptized until he was on his deathbed, and then by the Arian bishop Eusebius of Nicomedia, in the East. Interestingly, paintings of the legendary baptism of Constantine, including one in the Vatican Museum (Raphael Rooms), often show the interior of San Giovanni in Fonte.

In the right transept is the huge organ dating from the turn of the seventeenth century (the oldest organ in Rome), but the yellow pillars under the organ were taken from the Forum of Trajan, so they are from the early second century. Notice the tomb of Innocent III, who was the pope who met with St. Francis and gave him permission to begin the Franciscan order. For the pope who was perhaps the most powerful of all popes, it is a bit ironic that today his tomb is over the door to the gift shop. The sculpture above Innocent's tomb, depicting Christ between Saints Francis and Dominic (holding the rosary) is from the nineteenth century. Look for a painting of Francis meeting Innocent III, and one that shows a dream that Innocent III had in the year 1215 (just before the Fourth Lateran Council). In his dream he saw the church falling apart, and a man wearing rags (St. Francis) held up the church on his shoulders. The scene is also depicted in a cycle of frescoes on the walls of the upper church of San Francesco in Assisi.

The large statues of the apostles that line the nave are from the eighteenth century. Notice that Paul (not Matthias) replaces Judas as one of the twelve. The green columns in the statue niches are from the original

Constantinian church on this site. The red granite columns supporting the triumphal arch are also from the fourth-century basilica.

The Holy Door of San Giovanni is the first Holy Door, made for the jubilee of 1423. On one of the pillars toward the back of the basilica, there is a fragment of a fresco attributed to the artist Giotto, showing Pope Boniface VIII (bishop 1294–1303) proclaiming the first jubilee from the balcony of San Giovanni.

Finally, don't miss the cloister, which is another excellent example of a medieval cloister. This one was commissioned by Pope Innocent III and was built by the same family that did the cloister at San Paolo. Around the perimeter are artifacts, including the remnants of a fifth-century *cathedra*, said to be the oldest papal throne, as well as a red marble slab that was once venerated as the supposed surface on which Roman soldiers threw dice for Jesus' robe. Make sure to take some time for personal reflection and prayer in the cloister.

Prayer of St. John

(Lord Jesus) You are worthy to reveal the will of God and enforce it because you gave your life to save people of every race and nation for God
>
> And you have made them into a new people of ambassadors for God
> And they will share in your victory and in your Kingdom
> The Lamb of God who was crucified is now glorified
> You are worthy of all power and authority and lordship
> And all wisdom and honor and praise and blessing
> Blessing and honor and glory and sovereignty
> Belong to God the Father and to the Lamb of God forever
> Your works are great and wonderful
> Oh Lord, all-powerful God
> Your ways are true and righteous
> Oh King of all the nations
> Who would dare not glorify you, Oh Lord?
> For you alone are holy
> People of every nation will worship you in your presence
> Because your justice has been revealed
> Salvation comes from God and from the Lamb!

(The apostle John, adapted from the Book of Revelation, first century)

Rome

Prayer for the Intercession of St. John

Oh glorious Saint John, you were so loved by Jesus that you merited to rest your head upon his breast, and to be left in his place as a son to Mary. Pray for us to have a fervent love for Jesus and Mary. Let me be united with them now on earth and forever after in heaven . . .

    O Lord, shine the brightness of your light upon your church; that we, being illumined by the teaching of your apostle and evangelist John, may so walk in the light of your truth, that at length we may attain to the fullness of eternal life, through Jesus Christ our Lord, who lives and reigns with you and the Holy Spirit, one God, for ever and ever. Amen.

SAN PIETRO (PILGRIM CHURCH, PAPAL BASILICA)

Location

Usually known simply as "Saint Peter's," the basilica of St. Peter is located in the Vatican, which is now a country unto itself. The name *Vatican*, however, is pre-Christian and was originally the name of the area on the west side of the Tiber, north of Trastevere, which became known as the Vatican Hill. This was the site of the Circus of Nero, sometimes called the Circus of Caligula, since Caligula actually began construction of the Circus, though it was finished by Nero. In fact the obelisk in the Piazza San Pietro is from the Circus of Nero. It was put in its current place in 1585, as part of the construction of the new basilica. The project of moving it took one thousand workers almost one hundred days.

    It was in the Circus of Nero that the apostle Peter was crucified. The exact location of the Circus was running east-west along what is now the south side of the basilica, so that the site of Peter's martyrdom is now marked by the Altar of the Crucifixion of Peter, in the left transept of the basilica. Peter was buried in the necropolis along the north side of the Circus, or what is now directly underneath the basilica. The site of his tomb immediately became a place of pilgrimage, so that it was known throughout the Christian community, and its location was passed down from generation to generation. Apparently the area was marked off by a low retaining wall during the time of Anacletus (bishop 76–88), and a small shrine was built over the grave by Anicetus (bishop 155–166). Later, during the time that Zephyrinus was bishop (188–217), a priest named Gaius wrote that there was a monument (called a "trophy," the so-called "trophy of Gaius") on the site, built as a shrine and a marker for the visitation of pilgrims. This is probably a reference to the shrine built in the mid-second century.

San Pietro (St. Peter's Basilica) in the Vatican

The Story

According to tradition, the apostle Peter came to Rome in about 42 or 43 CE. However, he was at the meeting of apostles in Jerusalem that is mentioned in the book of Acts, which took place in about the year 50 CE. In any case, most accounts assume that Peter came to Rome before Paul, though Paul's letter to the Romans (written in about the year 57) gives no

Rome

indication that Paul knew Peter was in Rome. Peter is said to have stayed in the home of the senator Pudens and presided over the Eucharist in the house church of Pudenziana. Peter is traditionally given the title of the first bishop of Rome, and although the office of bishop and the papacy as we know it emerged over time, Peter's status as an apostle would most certainly give him the kind of authority that bishops would later have as "overseers." Peter must have already been in Rome when Paul arrived in chains in the year 60 CE. Both Paul and Peter were martyred during the persecution of the emperor Nero, probably in 65 CE, though some date Peter's death as late as 67. Since Paul was a Roman citizen, he was executed by beheading, but since Peter was not, he was crucified. According to tradition, Peter was crucified upside down, because he did not believe he was worthy to die in the same way that Jesus did, and he begged his executioners to kill him some other way (see John 21:18–19).

After being buried in the Vatican necropolis, the place of Peter's grave was venerated for two hundred years. There is a tradition that says that the body of St. Peter was temporarily transferred to the catacombs of San Sebastiano to protect it from the persecution of the emperor Valerian (reigned 253–260), who specifically targeted Christian burial sites. Archaeologists have confirmed that the remains of Peter were moved for a time, and then later returned, though at this time they were hidden within the wall of the trophy itself. This would have been some time before the turn of the fourth century. The bones of Peter were found in the wall in the early twentieth century, and can now be seen if one takes the tour of the Vatican Necropolis.

The Church

The emperor Constantine built the first basilica over the site of Peter's tomb. This was in fact the first basilica Constantine built, beginning construction in the year 320, and according to one legend, the emperor himself broke ground with his own bare hands, and carried twelve baskets of dirt—one for each apostle. The church was consecrated in 326, with a solid gold cross weighing 150 pounds (a gift from Constantine and his mother Helena) placed over the tomb. The building was finished in 349. Probably about the size of San Giovanni, it is also said to have held 3,500 people. In order to build the church directly over the tomb of Peter, Constantine had the necropolis (which was partly above ground at the time) cut down and filled in. Peter's tomb was (and still is) directly below the main altar. Today you can go below the floor of the present church to the Crypt of the Popes (the *Sacred Grottoes*), and there you are standing in the original Constantinian basilica. While in the Vatican Museum, look for the painting *Fire in the Borgo* (in the Sala del Incendio, the "Fire Room"). In the background of the painting you can see the façade of the original St. Peter's basilica.

Pope Damasus (bishop 366–383) commissioned a fountain for the basilica, with a huge bronze pinecone, which is now in the gardens of the Vatican Museums. In the year 595, Pope Gregory I (Gregory the Great, bishop 590–604) embellished the tomb and built a new altar over it. Charles the Great (Charlemagne) was crowned Holy Roman Emperor here at Christmas in the year 800. The red porphyry circle in the center of the nave is meant to mark the spot where the emperors of the Holy Roman Empire knelt to be crowned by the popes. After the Arab invasion in the ninth century, Pope Leo IV (bishop 847–855) enclosed the Vatican campus within a wall (now known as the Leonine Wall). The Vatican itself came to be known as the Leonine City. Pope Callistus II (bishop 1119–1124) further embellished the altar over Peter's tomb. Pope Nicholas III (bishop 1277–1280) lived in the Vatican, and after the return of the papacy from Avignon, the Vatican became the permanent residence of the popes, with the exception of the time the popes lived in the Quirinal Palace. Pope Nicholas V (bishop 1447–1455) created the residence that became the Vatican papal apartments.

In 1506, Pope Julius II (bishop 1503–1513) made the decision to tear down the old basilica and build a new one. The original design for the new basilica was by the architect Bramante, and was a Greek cross plan (meaning that the arms of the cross were the same length on all four sides). Work was begun, and in fact the first stone laid for the new basilica is now under one of the pillars supporting the dome (Veronica's Column). Some of the building material was taken from the Roman forum, and the rubble from the old basilica would be used to fill in the hollow spaces in some of the walls of the new church. Pope Julius also expanded the papal apartments, commissioning Raphael to decorate what are now the Raphael Rooms of the Vatican Museums. Pope Pius IV (bishop 1559–1565) enlarged and embellished the papal apartments even further.

The dome was designed by Michelangelo, though he would never see it completed. It took almost two years to put up and another twelve years to finish the exterior. It took over a century to finish the new basilica, in part because Rome was invaded again, this time by German Lutherans, in the early sixteenth century. In 1605 the decision was made to abandon Bramante's Greek cross plan, and change to a Latin cross (effectively lengthening the nave), probably so that the new basilica would hold more people. Construction was nearly complete when the façade was finished in 1612, and the new basilica was finally consecrated in 1626.

The piazza in front of the basilica was designed by Bernini, who had wanted the circular colonnade to close off the piazza completely. However, the last section was never built, which now leaves the welcoming "open arms" entrance from the Via della Conciliazione. Bernini would also create the *baldacchino* and the sculpture of *The Throne of Peter*, as well as the tomb of Pope Alexander VII (bishop 1655–1667), who had commissioned the piazza and the sculpture. While in the piazza, be sure to find the small circles in the pavement on each side. If you stand on the circle and look out toward the colonnade, the columns line up perfectly. If you walk away from the circle and watch the columns, they seem to open and close like louvers. This is more than a curiosity; it is evidence of the genius of Bernini's architecture and the skill of the builders. Finally, as you face the basilica, the fountain on the left is by Bernini, the one on the right is by the architect who created the façade.

The Façade of San Pietro, as Seen from Piazza San Pietro

The first Vatican council, Vatican I (1869–1870) was held in St. Peter's, the bishops seated in the right transept of the basilica. In the early twentieth century, the fascists took control of Italy, which resulted in the Lateran Treaty of 1929. This treaty made the Vatican a sovereign state, and led to the construction of the Via della Conciliazione. The second Vatican council, Vatican II (1962–1965) was also held here, with the bishops seated on either side along the nave.

What to Look For

The inscription on the façade of the basilica says: "In honor of the Prince of the Apostles (Peter), (dedicated by) Paul V Borghese, Roman Pontifex Maximus (Bishop of Rome) in the year 1612, the seventh year of his pontificate." Two imposing statues of Peter (with the keys) and Paul (with the sword) seem to stand guard over the basilica. As you enter the portico before entering the basilica, go to the right to see the equestrian statue of the emperor Constantine by Bernini. Presumably, Bernini sculpted Constantine as he was seeing the vision of the Chi-Rho, but put him on a horse like traditional depictions of St. Paul's conversion on the road to Damascus. By doing this, Bernini is making a comparison between the vision of Paul and the vision of Constantine. The statue is housed in an atrium, and unfortunately you won't be able to get very close, but it is still worth a look. As you step into the church, notice the parts of the threshold steps that are red marble. This marble comes from some of the columns of the original St. Peter's. One of the closed doors is called the Door of Death, which is only opened for a Pope's funeral procession.

As you enter the nave, stop to take in the scope of the space. The large inscriptions on the inside of the dome and transepts have letters that are about six feet tall. The inscriptions include the texts of Matthew 16:16–19 and John 21:15–17, concluding with the words, "Oh shepherd of the church, you feed all the lambs and sheep of Christ," which is repeated in Greek, and ending with, "From here one faith shines throughout the world, from here the unity of the priesthood originates."

Over the altar is Bernini's bronze *baldacchino*. Made in 1633, it weighs about eighty tons. It was made from the bronze beams taken from the portico of the Pantheon. The altar itself is made from an ancient stone slab taken from the Forum of Nerva.

Rome

San Pietro, Interior

On the right-hand side at the back of the church is Michelangelo's masterpiece, the *Pietá*. It is behind glass because in 1972, an insane person damaged it by hitting it with a hammer. Fortunately it was repaired, and from the vantage point of the other side of the bulletproof glass, you won't be able to see the difference. In spite of the attempt to destroy it, Michelangelo's *Pietá* is arguably the finest sculpture ever made by human hands. It is also unique in that Michelangelo himself signed it, in the sash across Mary's clothing. Michelangelo was only twenty-five years old when he created this.

As you go down the nave toward the apse, notice the old bronze statue of Peter on the right side. Theories vary on just how old this statue is, but it may have come from the original basilica. The halo over his head was added in more recent times. Note that Peter's right foot is worn down from the faithful who have touched it for centuries. There is a tradition that this statue is dressed in papal vestments every year on the feast of St. Peter (and Paul), June 29. These vestments include the papal triple crown, even though this has not been used by the popes since it was abandoned by Paul VI (bishop 1963–1978) on the grounds that the office of the papacy should be a ministry of service rather than a position of royalty.

The Churches of Rome

Statue of St. Helena, Church of San Pietro

The four corners of the dome are supported by four large statue niches, which are said to contain relics of the passion of Christ. According to tradition, these relics were once exposed for pilgrims to view but are now enclosed in the niches (or according to one source, in one of the niches). The niches themselves include pillars from the old basilica, as well as statues of saints who are in some way related to the relics. The four statues are St. Andrew, St. Veronica, St. Helena, and St. Longinus. There is a legend that says that Veronica used her veil to wipe the face of Jesus when he stumbled carrying the cross. Veronica's veil then became a relic, and is said to be kept in the niche above the statue of Veronica. The statue of Helena is the original, the copy of which is in the Chapel of St. Helena in the church of Santa Croce in Gerusalemme. You can see that the cross was added to the statue, which was probably originally a statue of a pagan goddess modified to become a statue of the emperor's mother. Helena is remembered as the one who found the True Cross in Jerusalem, and it is said that another fragment of the cross of Christ is also kept here in the niche. Longinus is the traditional name of the soldier

199

Rome

who pierced Christ's side with a spear to confirm that he was dead (John 19:34). According to the story, he was both a convert and a martyr. The spear was kept in the Holy Land and eventually given to Pope Innocent VIII (bishop 1484–1492) by the Sultan Bajazet in 1492 (the same year the *Titulus Crucis* was found). The spear is also said to be kept above the statue in the niche. The statue of St. Longinus is by Bernini.

Behind the altar is Bernini's bronze sculpture of *The Throne of Peter*. According to legend, the sculpture is built around an actual chair used by the apostle Peter. In reality, there is a chair in there, but it is a later papal *cathedra* made of wood and ivory, which was given to the pope by king Charles the Bald after his coronation as emperor in the year 875. The seventeenth-century sculpture shows the *cathedra* of papal authority held up by four early doctors of the church: St. Ambrose and St. Augustine

Bernini's Bronze Sculpture of The Throne of Peter, Church of San Pietro

(who are depicted wearing mitres), and St. Athanasius and St. John Chrysostom. Above the chair, we see the dove with rays of light, symbolizing the inspiration of the Holy Spirit. Thus papal authority is understood as being supported by tradition (the doctors of the church) and inspired by the Holy Spirit.

Below the altar is the tomb of Peter. You can see into the *confessio*, which was part of the original basilica, and there is an ancient mosaic of Christ that is still in its original position from the Constantinian church. Closest to the tomb of Peter is the small niche which holds the *pallia*, the white lamb's wool stoles that are given to archbishops by the pope. This symbolizes that the authority of a bishop is granted by the pope, providing the unity of the church worldwide, as well as the unity with the historic church of the martyrs.

In the baptistery, the baptismal font is actually a large porphyry sarcophagus lid. Along the length of the center of the nave, make sure to notice the marks on the floor showing the sizes of the other great churches of the world—all of them could fit within St. Peter's, and the Statue of Liberty could fit under the dome.

Be sure to go below into the Crypt of the Popes, not only to see the tombs of many of world's most beloved popes, but also to be in the space that was the original St. Peter's basilica. There is also a museum, though it may be closed on days when there is a papal audience. Finally, you can go up into the dome (you may have seen people up inside the inner drum of the dome). However, be warned—there are almost five hundred steps, and although you may be able to bypass some of the steps by taking an elevator, most of the climb is still by foot, and before you emerge into the open air on top, you will have to go through the cramped space between the walls of the dome. It is not for the claustrophobic, but if you brave the climb, you will be rewarded with spectacular views.

Prayer of St. Peter

Lord I come to you—you are a living stone, rejected by the world but chosen and precious in the sight of the Father. Make me a living stone, build me into a spiritual temple, where a holy priesthood will offer spiritual sacrifices acceptable to God through you. Amen

(The apostle Peter, adapted from his *First Letter*, first century.)

Rome

Prayer of Thanksgiving for All the Saints

We thank you oh God, for the saints of all ages. For those who in times of darkness kept the lamp of faith burning. For the great souls who saw visions of larger truth and dared to declare it. For the multitude of quiet and gracious souls whose presence has purified and sanctified the world. And for those known and loved by us, who have passed from this earthly fellowship into the fuller light of life with you. [*Take a moment to thank God for those loved ones who have passed on to eternal life.*] May we, who aspire to have part in their joy, be filled with the Spirit that blessed their lives, so that, having shared their faith on earth, we may also know their peace in your kingdom. Accept this, our thanksgiving, through Jesus Christ, to whom be praise and dominion forever. Amen.

Chapter 5

Walking Tours of Rome

TEN DAYS IN ROME

The ideal way to see the eternal city is to spend two weeks there and go at a relaxed pace. It is difficult to experience the city in less time, though it is understandable that many people will want to see other cities as well, especially on their first trip to Italy. Nevertheless, the city of Rome offers more than enough to spend your whole vacation there. If one were to see everything mentioned in this book, it would take at least ten to twelve days. The itinerary offered here is a version of the one I use when I take my students to Rome. The order of days is meant to get as close to a chronological tour of Rome as possible, without wasting time bouncing around the city. Thus the itinerary is organized according to location as much as chronology. The days can, of course, be rearranged but make sure to check that the sites listed are open on the days you plan to visit. I have not included specific days and times that sites and churches are open because they are subject to change, and it is expected that you will need to check the Internet or an annual guide book for the latest on those details. Churches especially are often closed in the afternoon, some as much as from noon to 4 p.m., so make sure to plan your days accordingly. In some cases, the opening and closing times will change depending on the month you are visiting. Also note that some museums and other sites are closed on Mondays.

Rome

It's best if you can leave enough time to see Rome on foot. Since the itineraries below are organized by area of the city, you should be able to walk almost everywhere. While the Rome metro is reliable and generally safe, it can be very crowded at certain times of the day—and you can't see Rome from underground. So plan to walk as much as possible. The exceptions to this are the catacombs, which may require taking a cab, since they are on the outskirts of the city (Priscilla on the north side, and the others to the south). The churches outside the walls may also take up more time in transit, so while San Paolo is near a metro stop, you may want to take a cab to San Lorenzo.

Finally, the pope conducts regular audiences which you can attend by arranging for a ticket ahead of time. The papal audiences are usually once a week when the pope is in Rome, and are held in Piazza San Pietro. While the papal audience can be a spiritually uplifting experience, be prepared to spend the better part of your afternoon in the piazza with thousands of people.

- ☐ *Day One*
  - ▶ Morning
    - Santi Cosma e Damiano
    - Roman Forum
    - Palatine Hill
  - ▶ Afternoon
    - Colosseum
    - Arch of Constantine
    - Ludus Magnus
    - Church of San Clemente
- ☐ *Day Two*
  - ▶ Morning
    - Imperial Fora (Forum of Caesar, Augustus, Trajan)
    - Markets of Trajan (May be closed on Mondays)
    - Capitoline Hill and Capitoline Museums
    - Largo Argentina
  - ▶ Afternoon
    - Pantheon
    - Piazza Navona
    - Church of Sant' Agostino
- ☐ *Day Three*

- Morning
  - Church of Santa Sabina
  - Circus Maximus
  - Temples of the Forum Boarium
  - Church of Santa Maria in Cosmedin
- Afternoon
  - Lunch in Trastevere
  - Church of Santa Maria in Trastevere
  - Church of Santa Cecilia
  - Church of San Benedetto (May be closed on Mondays)

☐ Day Four
- Morning
  - Catacombs of Priscilla (May be closed on Mondays)
- Afternoon
  - Catacombs of San Callisto (May be closed on Wednesdays)
  - Catacombs of San Sebastiano
  - Catacombs of Domitilla (May be closed on Tuesdays)

☐ Day Five
- Morning
  - Piazza della Republica/Baths of Diocletian
  - Church of Santa Maria degli Angeli
  - National Museum at the Baths of Diocletian (Therme)
- Afternoon
  - Church of Santa Maria Maggiore
  - Church of Santa Pudenziana
  - Church of Santa Prassede
  - Church of San Pietro in Vincoli

☐ Day Six
- Morning
  - Trevi Fountain
  - Capuchin Cemetery
  - Castel Sant' Angelo
  - Lunch in the Castle
- Afternoon
  - Piazza di Spagna and Spanish Steps
  - Shopping along the Via del Corso

Rome

- Piazza del Popolo and Piazza Napoleone
- Church of Santa Maria del Popolo

☐ *Day Seven*
- ▶ Morning
  - San Giovanni in Laterano (with baptistery and Holy Stairs)
  - Church of Santa Croce in Gerusalemme
- ▶ Afternoon
  - Church of San Paolo Fuori le Mura

☐ *Day Eight*
- ▶ Morning
  - Vatican Necropolis (special appointment needed)
  - Piazza San Pietro and St. Peter's Basilica
- ▶ Afternoon
  - Free time for exploring and shopping in the Vatican

☐ *Day Nine*
- ▶ Morning
  - San Lorenzo Fuori le Mura
- ▶ Afternoon
  - Vatican Museums and Sistine Chapel

☐ *Day Ten*
- ▶ Free Day, or other optional sites:
  - Day trip to Ostia
  - Baths of Caracalla

ONE WEEK IN ROME

If you have one week in Rome, that is plenty of time to see the most important things, but not enough time to see everything on the list, so the trick will be to set aside some things for the next trip (and you will want to come back). The one week itinerary offered here is based on my own personal opinions on what are the most important sites to see and things to do in Rome.

☐ *Day One*
- ▶ Morning

- Santi Cosma e Damiano
- Roman Forum
- Palatine Hill
▶ Afternoon
- Colosseum
- Arch of Constantine
- Ludus Magnus
- Church of San Clemente

☐ *Day Two*
▶ Morning
- Imperial Fora (Forum of Caesar, Augustus, Trajan)
- Markets of Trajan (May be closed on Mondays)
- Capitoline Hill and Capitoline Museums
- Largo Argentina
▶ Afternoon
- Pantheon
- Piazza Navona
- Church of Sant' Agostino

☐ *Day Three*
▶ Morning
- Church of Santa Sabina
- Circus Maximus
- Temples of the Forum Boarium
- Church of Santa Maria in Cosmedin
▶ Afternoon
- Lunch in Trastevere
- Church of Santa Maria in Trastevere
- Church of Santa Cecilia
- Church of San Benedetto (May be closed on Mondays)

☐ *Day Four*
▶ Morning—*Depending on the day of the week, choose one:*
- Catacombs of Priscilla (May be closed on Mondays)
- Catacombs of San Callisto (May be closed on Wednesdays)
- Catacombs of Domitilla (May be closed on Tuesdays)
▶ Afternoon
- Church of Santa Pudenziana

Rome

- Church of Santa Prassede
- Church of Santa Maria Maggiore

☐ *Day Five*
  ▶ Morning
    - Trevi Fountain
    - Capuchin Cemetery
    - Castel Sant' Angelo
    - Lunch in the Castle
  ▶ Afternoon
    - Piazza di Spagna and Spanish Steps
    - Shopping along the Via del Corso
    - Piazza del Popolo and Piazza Napoleone
    - Church of Santa Maria del Popolo

☐ *Day Six*
  ▶ Morning
    - Church of Santa Croce in Gerusalemme
    - San Giovanni in Laterano (with baptistery and Holy Stairs)
  ▶ Afternoon
    - Church of San Paolo Fuori le Mura

☐ *Day Seven*
  ▶ Morning
    - Piazza San Pietro and St. Peter's Basilica
  ▶ Afternoon
    - Vatican Museums and Sistine Chapel

FOUR DAYS IN ROME

Many people plan a vacation in Italy that includes only a few days in Rome. While that is not ideal, I will offer an itinerary that will allow you to accomplish as much as possible. However, you will notice that the Vatican Museums and the Sistine Chapel are not included. I know that most people feel that the Sistine Chapel is a must see, however that's because they often don't know what else Rome has to offer, and they don't realize just how much time it will take to get through the Vatican Museums to the Sistine Chapel, not to mention the fact that most people who do get to see the Sistine Chapel will tell you that it is not a very spiritual experience. The itinerary below may be a bit more ambitious than you will want, so feel free to pick and choose. If you find yourself in Rome for a very short time, and perhaps want to limit your visit to that part of the city nearest your hotel, note that these itineraries are organized by area, so concentrate on the day(s) with the sites closest to where you are staying.

- ☐ Day One
  - ▶ Morning
    - Santi Cosma e Damiano
    - Roman Forum
    - Palatine Hill
  - ▶ Afternoon
    - Colosseum
    - Arch of Constantine
    - Ludus Magnus
    - Church of San Clemente
- ☐ Day Two
  - ▶ Morning
    - Pantheon
    - Piazza Navona
    - Capitoline Hill and Capitoline Museums
  - ▶ Afternoon
    - Lunch in Trastevere
    - Church of Santa Maria in Trastevere
    - Church of Santa Cecilia
    - Church of San Benedetto (May be closed on Mondays)
- ☐ Day Three
  - ▶ Morning—*Depending on the day of the week, choose one:*
    - Catacombs of Priscilla (May be closed on Mondays)
    - Catacombs of San Callisto (May be closed on Wednesdays)
    - Catacombs of Domitilla (May be closed on Tuesdays)
  - ▶ Afternoon
    - Church of Santa Maria Maggiore
    - Church of Santa Prassede
    - Church of Santa Pudenziana

Rome

- *Day Four*
  - ▸ Morning
    - Piazza San Pietro and St. Peter's Basilica
  - ▸ Afternoon
    - Church of San Paolo Fuori le Mura

OTHER CHURCHES WORTH VISITING

If you are fortunate enough to be in Rome for an extended period of time, here is a list of additional churches that are worth seeing.

- ☐ San Vitale (Title Church)—Note the original fifth-century façade below street level
- ☐ San Marco (Title Church)
- ☐ Santa Susanna (Title Church)
- ☐ San Crisogono (Title Church)
- ☐ San Lorenzo in Lucina (Title Church)
- ☐ Quattro Coronati (Title Church)
- ☐ Santi Giovanni e Paolo (Title Church)—Has Roman house underneath
- ☐ San Silvestro e Martino ai Monte (Title Church)
- ☐ Santo Stefano Rotondo
- ☐ Santa Maria Sopra Minerva
- ☐ Santa Maddelena
- ☐ Santa Costanza (Constantinian Mausoleum)
- ☐ Sant' Agnese Fuori le Mura—Has a small catacomb which may be open
- ☐ Santa Maria in Domnica (also known as Navicella)
- ☐ Santa Maria della Vittoria—Has Bernini's *Ecstasy of St. Teresa*
- ☐ San Francesco a Ripa—Has Bernini's statue of *Blessed Ludovica Albertoni*
- ☐ San Luigi dei Francesi—Has Caravaggio's St. Matthew cycle
- ☐ Santi Ambrosio e Carlo al Corso

Walking Tours of Rome

- ☐ Chiesa Nuova
- ☐ San Teodoro (now a Greek Orthodox church)
- ☐ San Lorenzo in Damaso (at Palazzo Cancelleria)
- ☐ Santa Maria in Aracoeli
- ☐ *Some other sites worth a visit*
    - ▶ The Baths of Caracalla
    - ▶ Villa Borghese/Borghese Gallery
    - ▶ Panoramic view of the city from the top of the Victor Emmanuel Monument

Appendix A

Coming Back to the Twenty-First Century

USING THIS BOOK AS A DEVOTIONAL AID AFTER YOUR TRIP

MY HOPE IS THAT this book will be of ongoing help to you, long after your trip to Rome. In fact, I hope you make many trips to Rome. However, even when you are not in Rome, I encourage you to use the book as an aid to prayer. As you look at the pictures and perhaps reread parts of the book, remember being in these holy places, and bring that feeling back in your prayers. Continue to use the prayers given here, and look for others like them, to maintain a rewarding prayer life. Also, use the photographs on the companion website, www.Romesick.org, to bring yourself back to what it felt like to be on holy ground.

If you find this book and your trip to Rome particularly uplifting, please send me your thoughts, feelings, and any stories you would like to share. With your permission, I may post them on the book's website, www.Romesick.com, to encourage the faith of others along the way.

Appendix A

SUGGESTIONS FOR FURTHER READING

Other Books by the Author

For more information on the persecution of Christians, as well as the book of Revelation in the early church, see:

The Wedding of the Lamb: A Historical Approach to the Book of Revelation by James L. Papandrea

(The prayer of St. John adapted from the book of Revelation that appears in this book is from the appendix, "The Book of Revelation in Plain English" in *Wedding of the Lamb*.)

For more information on the early church in general, see:

Reading the Early Church Fathers: From the Didache to the Council of Nicaea by James L. Papandrea

For more on prayer and the spiritual life, see:

Spiritual Blueprint: How We Live, Work, Love, Play and Pray by James L. Papandrea

For more information on the author, visit:

www.JimPapandrea.com

Other Books You Should Read

If you're interested in a deeper understanding of the church in Rome in the early centuries of Christianity, here is a list of other books I recommend:

- *The Confessions* by St. Augustine of Hippo
- *Early Christian Literature: Christ and Culture in the 2nd and 3rd Centuries* by Helen Rhee
- *Paul the Martyr* by David L. Eastman
- *The Second Church: Popular Christianity A.D. 200–400* by Ramsay MacMullen
- *Perpetua's Passion: The Death and Memory of a Young Roman Woman* by Joyce E. Salisbury
- *Conflict at Rome: Social Order and Hierarchy in Early Christianity* by James S. Jeffers
- *Understanding Early Christian Art* by Robin Jensen
- *Subterranean Rome* by L. V. Rutgers
- *The Bones of St. Peter* by John Evangelist Walsh
- *Signs and Mysteries* by Mike Aquilina

Appendix B

Chart: Rome Timeline

BCE (BC)

753   Mythical Founding of the City of Rome by Twins Romulus and Remus

509   Beginning of the Roman Republic, Rule Changes from Kings to Senate

44   Julius Caesar Assassinated

31   Battle of Actium: Octavian Defeats Marc Antony and Cleopatra

29   Octavian Given the Name *Augustus*, End of the Republic

6/5   Jesus Christ Born in Bethlehem

2   Augustus Proclaimed *Pater Patriae*, Father of the Country

CE (AD)

41   Emperor Caligula Assassinated in the Cryptoporticus on the Palatine

42   (According to Tradition) the Apostle Peter Arrives in Rome

50   Both Peter and Paul are in Jerusalem for a Meeting of the Apostles

52   Emperor Claudius Expels Jews from Rome (Probably Not Including Slaves)

Appendix B

57	The Apostle Paul Writes His Letter to the Romans
60	The Apostle Paul Arrives in Rome (Under House Arrest)
64	Great Fire of Rome (July 18–19), Probably Started by Emperor Nero
65	The Apostles Paul and Peter Martyred (Their Feast Day is June 29)
70	Siege of Jerusalem, Titus Enters the City and Destroys the Temple
79	Titus Becomes Emperor, Mt. Vesuvius Erupts Burying Pompeii
80	Colosseum Completed
95	Persecution of the Emperor Domitian, John Exiled to Patmos
96	Domitilla Martyred
110	Ignatius of Antioch Martyred in Rome
126	Martyrdom of St. Sabina (August 29), The Pantheon Rebuilt
165	Martyrdom of the Apologist Justin Martyr in Rome
202	Emperor Severus Issues Edict Authorizing Persecution of Christians
203	Arch of Severus Dedicated, Martyrdom of Perpetua et al. in Carthage
235?	Martyrdom of Saint Cecilia (November 22)
250	Persecution of the Emperor Decius
257/8	Persecution of the Emperor Valerian
258	Martyrdom of Sixtus II and Deacons, Including St. Lawrence (August 10)
287	Martyrdom of Saints Cosma and Damiano (September 27)
303	Diocletian and Galerius Begin the Great Persecution
305	Baths of Diocletian Built, Diocletian Retires
312	Battle at the Milvian Bridge (October 28): Constantine Defeats Maxentius
313	Edict of Milan: Constantine Legalizes Christianity
325	First Ecumenical Council: Nicaea
387	Death of St. Monica (Mother of St. Augustine) at Ostia
410	Gothic Invasion (Visigoths), Sack of Rome
431	Ecumenical Council of Ephesus Confirms Mary as "Mother of God"

Chart: Rome Timeline

451/2	Attila the Hun is Bribed to Leave Rome by Pope Leo I
455	Invasion of the Vandals in Rome
547	Invasion of the Ostrogoths in Rome
590	Pope Gregory the Great's Vision of the Angel Sheathing the Sword
595	Pope Gregory the Great Builds Embellished Altar over St. Peter's Tomb
609	Visit of the Emperor Phocas, Pantheon Converted into a Church
846/7	Arab Invasion—Major Basilicas Outside the Walls Ransacked
1084	War Between the Germans and Normans Comes to Rome
1309	Papacy Removed to Avignon
1377	Gregory XI Brings Papacy Back to Rome, Resulting in Two Rival Popes
1409	Attempt to Consolidate Papacy Back to One Pope Results in Three Popes
1417	Council of Constance Succeeds in Restoring Papacy (Martin V)
1475	Michelangelo born (died 1564)
1527	German Lutherans Invade Rome
1561	Michelangelo Turns the Baths of Diocletian into Santa Maria degli Angeli
1572	Caravaggio born (died 1610)
1598	Gian Lorenzo Bernini Born (died 1680)
1823	Fire Destroys San Paolo Fuori le Mura (St. Paul Outside the Walls)
1870	Unification of Italy
1929	Lateran Treaty Makes Vatican City a Sovereign State
1978	Author Jim Papandrea Arrives in Rome for the First Time at Age Fifteen

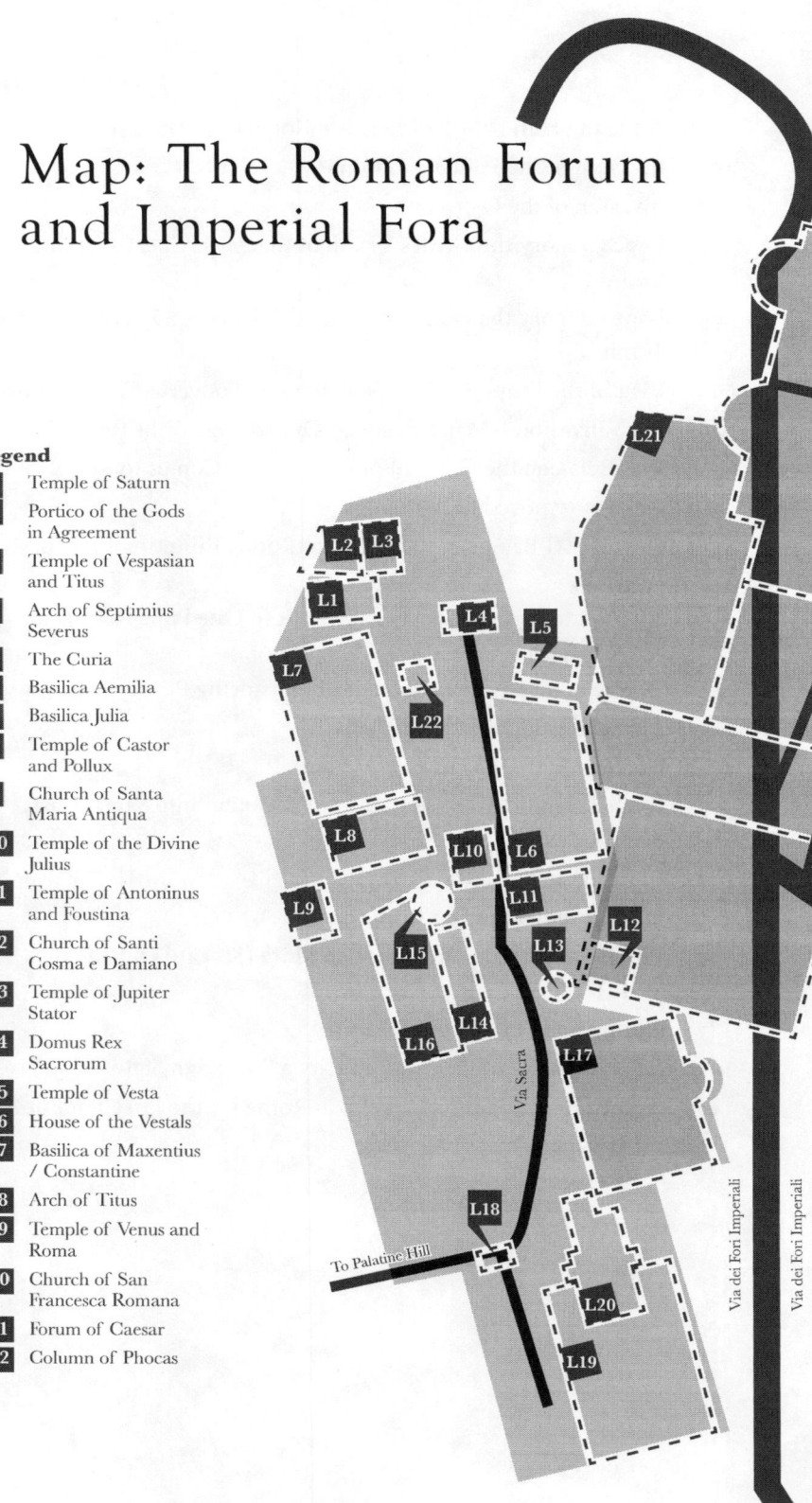

Map: The Roman Forum and Imperial Fora

Legend

- L1 Temple of Saturn
- L2 Portico of the Gods in Agreement
- L3 Temple of Vespasian and Titus
- L4 Arch of Septimius Severus
- L5 The Curia
- L6 Basilica Aemilia
- L7 Basilica Julia
- L8 Temple of Castor and Pollux
- L9 Church of Santa Maria Antiqua
- L10 Temple of the Divine Julius
- L11 Temple of Antoninus and Foustina
- L12 Church of Santi Cosma e Damiano
- L13 Temple of Jupiter Stator
- L14 Domus Rex Sacrorum
- L15 Temple of Vesta
- L16 House of the Vestals
- L17 Basilica of Maxentius / Constantine
- L18 Arch of Titus
- L19 Temple of Venus and Roma
- L20 Church of San Francesca Romana
- L21 Forum of Caesar
- L22 Column of Phocas

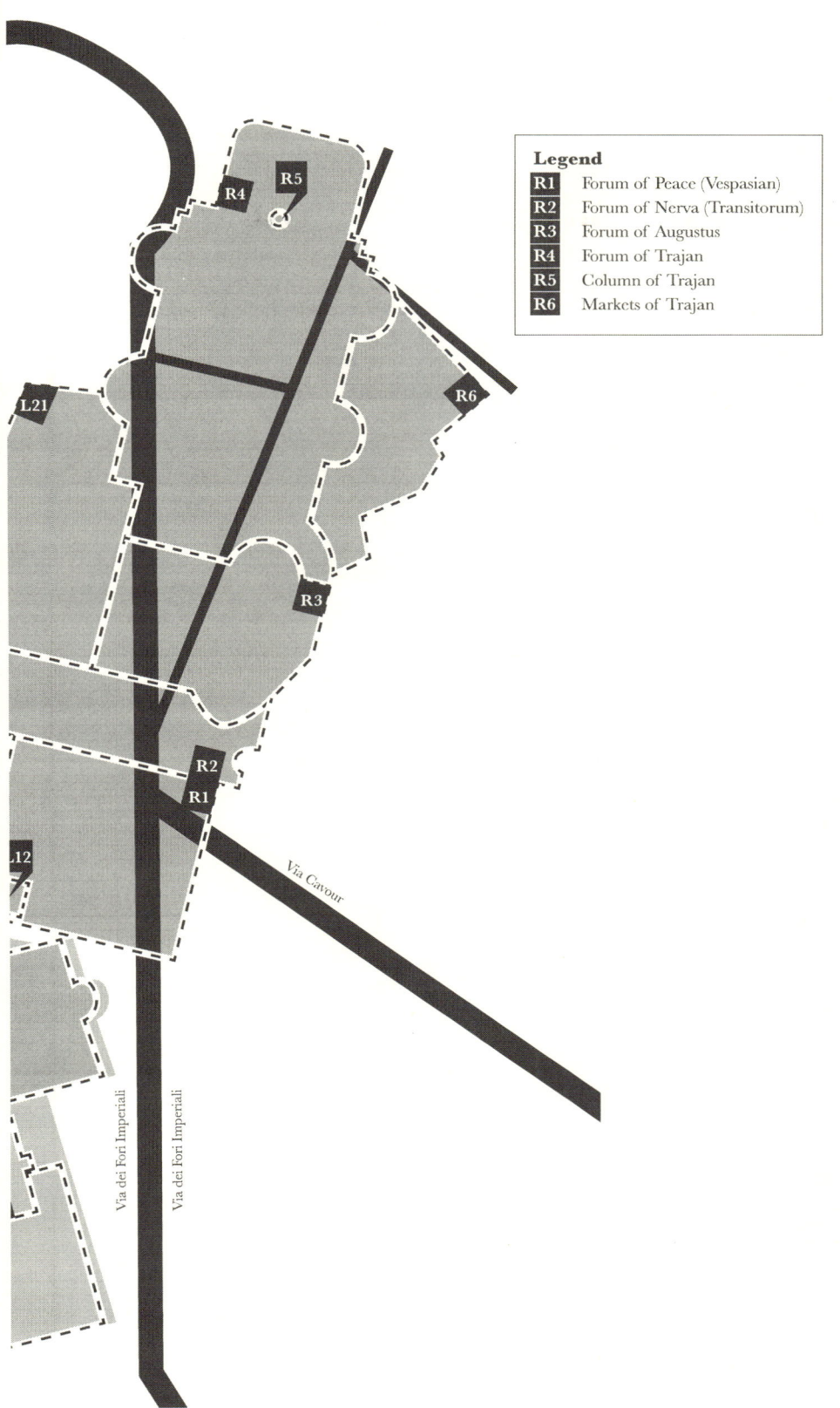

Map: The Churches of Rome and Other Important Sites

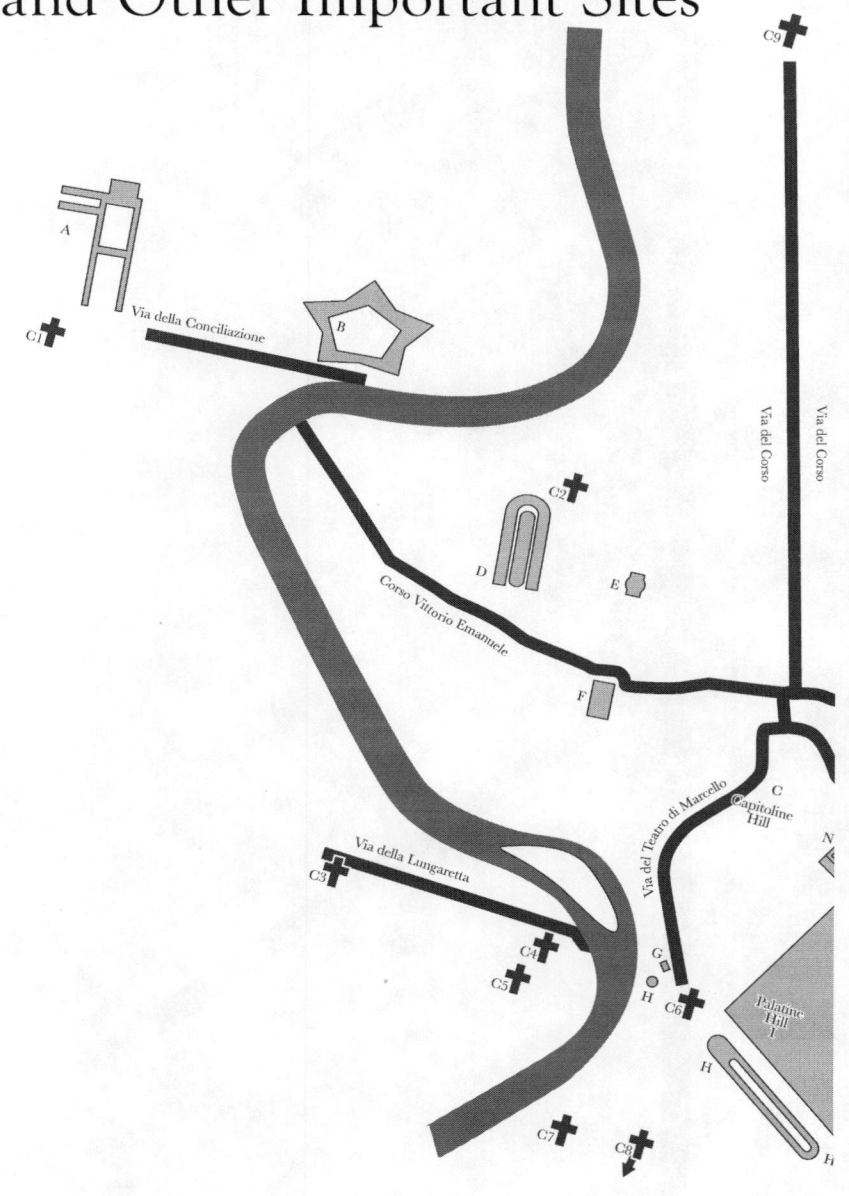

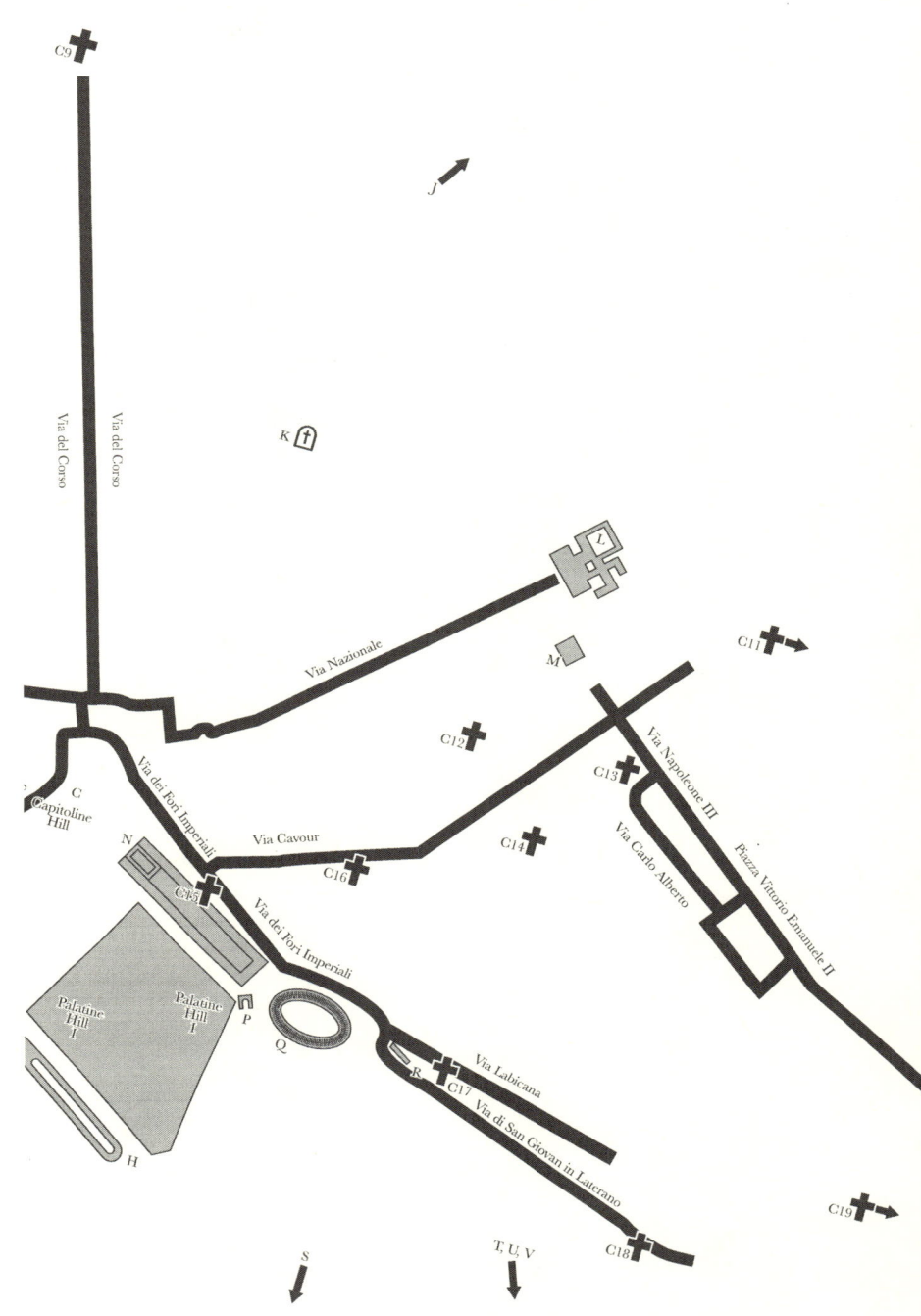

Sites

A	The Vatican Museums / Sistine Chapel
B	Castel Sant' Angelo
C	Capitoline Hill
D	Piazza Navona
E	The Pantheon
F	Largo Argentina
G	Temple of Hurcules
H	Temple of Portuna
I	Palatine Hill
J	The Catacombs of Priscilla
K	The Capuchin Cemetery
L	Baths of Diocletian / Santa Maria degli Angeli
M	National Museum at the Bahs of Diocletian
N	Roman Forum
P	The Arch of Constantine
Q	The Colosseum
R	The Ludus Magnus
S	Baths of Caracalla
T	Catacombs of San Callisto
U	Catacombs of Domitilla
V	Catacombs and Church of San Sebastiano

Churches

C1	San Pietro
C2	Sant' Agostino
C3	Santa Maria in Trastevere
C4	San Benedetto
C5	Santa Cecilia
C6	Santa Maria in Cosmedin
C7	Santa Sabina
C8	San Paolo Fuori le Mura
C9	Santa Maria del Popolo
C11	San Lorenzo Fuori le Mura
C12	Santa Pudenziana
C13	Santa Maria Maggiore
C14	Santa Prassede
C15	Santi Cosma e Damiano
C16	San Pietro in Vincoli
C17	San Clemente
C18	San Giovanni in Laterano
C19	Santa Croce in Gerusalemme